Architecture as Metaphor

Writing **Architecture**

A project of the Anyone Corporation

Earth Moves: The Furnishing of Territories
Bernard Cache, 1995
Architecture as Metaphor: Language, Number, Money
Kojin Karatani, 1995

The MIT Press   Cambridge, Massachusetts   London, England

Architecture as Metaphor
Language, Number, Money

Kojin Karatani translated by Sabu Kohso

edited by Michael Speaks

Translation from the Japanese was made possible by a grant from the Graham Foundation for Advanced Studies in the Fine Arts.

This book was printed and bound in the United States of America.

Library of Congress Cataloging-in-Publication Data

Karatani, Kōjin, 1941–
[In'yū to shite no kenchiku. English]
Architecture as metaphor : language, number, money / Kojin Karatani ; translated by Sabu Kohso ; edited by Michael Speaks.
p. cm. — (Writing architecture)
Includes bibliographical references.
ISBN 0-262-61113-9 (pbk. : alk. paper)
I. Speaks, Michael. II. Title. III. Series.
AC146.K321313 1995
895.6′45—dc20   95-18602
                                                  CIP

Kojin Karatani began his career as a literary critic in Japan; both of his works so far translated into English, *Origins of Modern Japanese Literature* and the present volume, *Architecture as Metaphor*, were originally published in literary journals. Karatani once told me with a wry smile that the first editions of this book were displayed in the science/engineering section of some bookstores and took a while to be relocated into the literature/philosophy section. Even though his official status is "literary critic," he tackles issues from a broad spectrum of domains including philosophy, logic, political economy, cultural anthropology, sociology, and urban studies. I assume that bookshops having trouble categorizing *Architecture as Metaphor* might have placed it according to the title; architecture is often included in the science/engineering (rather than culture) section in Japan.

In a roundabout way this episode sheds light on Karatani's idiosyncratic stance. He is totally indifferent to the territorialities of today's scholastic subjects, which, though categorized arbitrarily, nevertheless have ended up constructing their own ivory towers and forming immutable and untrespassable boundaries; his writing traverses these boundaries as if they never existed. Unlike many multidisciplinary generalists who travel the horizontal strata, he trans-

gresses categories by using his questioning to dig vertically through each domain while at the same time
remaining within it. His procedure is consistent to the
point of being violent; it is like a practice of pure radi-
calism. I cannot help but believe that he has a faith that
some sort of original exists deep down. In *Origins of
Modern Japanese Literature*, he attempts to reveal how
the modern nation-state called Japan has been constructed as an aesthetic fiction by way of literature; he
unearths "Japan" by elaborating conceptual devices such
as landscape, interiority, confession, illness, childhood,
and composition. Likewise, in *Architecture as Metaphor*
he excavates architecture down to the depths where the
original resides. This "architecture" of Karatani is irrelevant to the building-as-concrete-edifice that concerns
architects and it cannot be located in the science/engi-
neering section, despite the title. However, I believe
that because of this very uncategorizability, Karatani's
architecture will become an incentive for architects to
rethink architecture in an alternative manner and will
establish a strong rapport with architects themselves,
particularly in today's climate where architectural discourses are confronting serious crises on all fronts. In
this introduction I shall attempt to map the crises, and
by so doing I hope to map how the role of architecture
that Karatani extracts might be further contextualized.

Karatani treats architecture as a metaphor—that is,
the will to construct—and as a system where various
formalizations take place. In this sense architecture is
the name of the mechanism through which the metaphysics that ground Western thought inevitably came
into existence. In order to access this concept residing at
the bottom he proceeds to critique Platonism and
Marxism, to dismantle and tear apart the vulgarized
"isms" into their original fragments of events. To per-

form the procedure, enter Gödel and Wittgenstein to play the role of conceptual device for dismemberment. In the end, Plato and Marx are extracted and stripped bare: Plato, who is obsessed with the "will to architecture, . . . attributed as it is to the weak," and Marx, in love with commodities that endlessly repeat their "fatal leap." Here I detect Karatani's deep sympathy for beings who are continuously compelled to engage in desperate communications with the other. This aspect of Karatani seems to me to be related to Gianni Vattimo's "weak thought" and Massimo Cacciari's "negative thought." When the architectural discourse distilled from this connection is introduced into the context of the worldwide crises of architecture, I believe it will begin to play an important role.

It is not so much that architecture is now in crisis, but rather that ever since it came to be named "modern architecture" it has been in constant crisis. My observation has been that crises recur in large waves at hundred-year intervals, and we are now at the beginning of the third wave. The first appeared in the late eighteenth century. Until then, all architectural discourses had revolved around Vitruvius's *Ten Books on Architecture*, and it is not too much to say that the work of the architect was meant to fill the margins of this Vitruvian writing, which assumed the status of a Book. It was believed to offer a foundation for architectural thought in the language of classicism—a role similar to that played by the Bible for religious thought.

The beginning of the crisis was signaled when architects' belief in the Book began to waver. The age of world travel had arrived, and knowledge about the different architectural styles of different civilizations—such as the Orient—had been introduced. As archaeological knowledge expanded, the features of prehistoric architecture gradually came into view. What shocked the architects of the time most was that the actual architecture of ancient Greece was different from the one described and regarded as the prototype in Vitruvius's Book. It became apparent that the classical world had actually been an enclosed entity and that numerous worlds with different senses of time and space had existed external to it. This also meant that the architectural norm presented by Vitruvius had not really been the one and only universal principle, but only one of many architectures; in this manner classical architectural language was inevitably relativized. To deal with this situation, architects dislodged the Book from the place it had once occupied, leaving a vacant position. Then, by picking up various architectural languages, they constructed a new paradigm of "projects"—both design and theory—which were to rewrite the margins of the Book and in effect form a "supplement." This supplement—what might be called "architectural writing"—produced as many "one and only" images as there were projects to fill the vacant position; however, no single image became the definitive one. And paradoxically, only upon the fulfillment of such a project could one qualify as an Architect. Later, this vacant position was institutionalized and came to be called Art. In the nineteenth century this institution was guaranteed by the state. Hegel called architecture the mother of all arts; architecture was deemed autonomous and inclusive of all other fields such as music, fine art, and theater performance. On the other hand, this Art that was being constituted with state support virtually formed a meta-concept beyond these divisions and became a superior social institution. Thereafter every single architect's project had to be acknowledged by reference to the concept of art; architecture became "Architecture as Art." The pattern of practice wherein artists incessantly project their work into the vacant position was newly established in the modern period. In Karatani's speculation, this conceptual movement of art is similar to the movement of capital: it survives only by indefinitely postponing its end/settlement. And all of this is, after all, only an attempt to avoid the large wave by producing and manipulating small ones.

The concept of Art that supports architects' projects, however, was frail, and the Book of Vitruvius had to be constantly invoked. Furthermore, after the concept of Art became a state institution, it began to be oppressive. It was at this moment that utopia was summoned to inspire a positive prospect for the vacant position. Utopia is literally a place of nowhere; however, ideal images and progressive movements can be projected onto it. In order to induce utopia to ascend to the vacant position, Art, the erstwhile occupant, had to be removed: this marked the advent of the second crisis of architecture in the late nineteenth century. Gottfried Semper, Otto Wagner, and Adolf Loos proposed a new strategy to overcome the crisis—to attack the institution of art with architectural discourses and end the marriage of art and architecture. In their methodological procedure, building is analytically decomposed into four elements that are then reorganized according to "necessity." This process deprives architecture of all excess decoration and reduces it to a skeletal structure, stating above all else that architecture has nothing to do with art and should only be construction. The problematic of "Architecture as Construction" was thus acknowledged as the orientation to overcome the second crisis.

Architects reread this necessity-oriented methodology as the way to construct a utopia. Here, architectural writings *as projects* were focused on constructing architecture as utilitarian entities and accelerating the progressive movement toward utopia. There was a logical contradiction inherent in this avant-garde movement: although utopia technically exists nowhere, only projects that presented a concrete image of utopia were approved. Moreover, as soon as a visualized image is presented it becomes socially actual and should no longer, by definition, be called utopia, and yet it is still "utopian" because it is unrealizable inasmuch as it contains socially unbuildable conditions. After the mid-twentieth century, modernism began to encircle the world and the architectural and urban images once projected as utopian began to fill real space. In the 1960s this reached a saturation point; utopia was, ironically, realized. That is to say that the original utopia vanished and the avant-garde movements progressing toward it were inevitably terminated. The cultural revolutions in 1968 marked the date; since then, architects have been left with a "loss of subject"—the disappearance of the grand narrative. This should be deemed a new kind of crisis, the one in which we are living today—the third wave.

My book *The Dissolution of Architecture* (1975) was an attempt to survey these crises; it was planned as I sensed the commencement of this latest one. It scrutinized the syndrome in which, after the disappearance of utopia, architects would lose the *telos* that had provided their subjects, and proposed that the real subject should be "the absence of subject." Thus, while I began to restructure architectural design as a fabric of quotations, I also began to think that the concept of Architecture with a capital A still existed somewhere behind the textuality that allowed the quotation and that it was necessary to locate its binding power. In the West, where the concept of Art with a capital A had already been placed in the central category of cultural domains, Architecture was encouraged to join. Thus in the West the two—Art and Architecture—were once closely identified, but it subsequently became apparent that Architecture as Construction—the utopian project—had supplanted Architecture as Art. In contrast, in Japan architectural problematics could never have arisen in the same way. A firmly rooted tradition regards art as no more than a decoration of everyday life. The modern belief that a building is constructed as a "project" has never been acknowledged. It is precisely this tendency that allowed the sudden blossoming of the peculiar postmodernism of the 1980s. There was (and still is) a lack of criticality; buildings and cities were composed recklessly only by a textuality without subject. In Japan, from the beginning, Architecture with a capital A never existed.

When Karatani's *Architecture as Metaphor* was published in Japan, I was extremely interested in the fact that this book located the place of Architecture, the presence I felt behind textuality; and then I was struck by the procedures it uses to deconstruct the processes through which architecture is employed as metaphor. I think that *Architecture as Metaphor*, rather than remaining just a title, will begin to function as a double metaphor for architecture today: while it is still burdened with its old metaphorical power, it is now confronting the new crisis and oriented toward an unforeseen problematic formation. In this book, the logical scheme of how Architecture with a capital A can collapse is breathtakingly staged.

The work named "Kojin Karatani" continues to be produced in Japan, on a solitary island, by this figure of singular being, *der Einzige*. The place is always enclosed by its peculiar conditions, which are totally different from those of the West. In Japan, as Karatani himself claims, one has to play a double role to be fully critical;

this situation is not unfamiliar to me, as my work is framed by a double set of constraints as well. We have to engage in the critique of Japan, and also of the world outside. If one cannot fully construct the double-faceted stance, one's work will never escape the confines of the solitary island. In this work of Karatani, one of the key concepts is the intercourse with the exterior space, which, I believe, derives from his decision to engage in a permanent struggle with the enclosure called Japan.

As the twentieth century comes to a close, the whereabouts of the architectural crisis are becoming clearer. That is to say that after the disappearance of utopia, architecture stripped bare is being rediscovered in the place utopia used to be. Now the postutopian critique of architecture is paving the way for the extension of problematics into different dimensions. As for recent works confronting this new phase, I can think of Denis Hollier's *Against Architecture* and Mark Wigley's *Derrida's Haunt: The Architecture of Deconstruction*. The former criticizes Architecture as an anthropomorphic system with reference to Bataille, and the latter dissects the concept of Architecture hiding behind quotidian thinking through the analysis of Derrida. Karatani's *Architecture as Metaphor*, though it descends from a totally different lineage, attempts to directly grasp the core of the same crisis by a tireless retrospection of the origin. After weathering the first two waves that have arrived in hundred-year cycles—first with Architecture as Art and then with Architecture as Construction—it seems to me that *Architecture as Metaphor* points out a way to overcome our present crisis.

Arata Isozaki

On the English Edition of *Architecture as Metaphor*

Architecture as Metaphor is Karatani's most resolute attempt to confront the metaphysical mechanism that has tacitly normalized the intellectual practices of the West ever since Plato's time. By an exhaustive analysis of the ways in which architecture as metaphor pervades our thinking in various domains—philosophy, literature, city planning, linguistics, cultural anthropology, political economy, psychoanalysis, and mathematics— this book means to undermine the overcharged and even perverse constraining power of the figure of "architecture as metaphor." There are five major essays that follow the same line of pursuit: "Marx: The Center of His Possibilities" (1974); "Introspection and Retrospection" (1980); "Architecture as Metaphor" (1981); "Language, Number, Money" (1983); and "Researches" (1985– present); all were later published in collections of essays of the same title, except for "Language, Number, Money," which was included in *Introspection and Retrospection* (1985), and "Researches," which was published in two parts (*Researches I* [1986] and *II* [1989]).

In his essay published as a postscript to *Introspection and Retrospection*, Akira Asada spoke of the three central essays in this series in terms of "A Document of Wars" or, more particularly, "a document of battles lost." According to Asada, this work is an attempt to "escape the enclosed sphere of metaphysics, . . . but not by relying on a specific rhetoric within a restricted domain, like, for instance, the strategy of Derrida." Instead it is executed "in a more general field which opens itself up by penetrating through every discipline." Asada continues:

[It would be] unlikely if such a reckless, direct confrontation with the largest and strongest enemy would win an immediate success; on the contrary, the march is full of obstacles—no sooner does it seem to progress than a moment of stagnation arrives. The same approach is repeated time and again with only slight strategical shifts in nuance; as soon as a new escape route is discovered, it has to be abandoned. Repeating these countless flights, the author tirelessly restarts his assault from ever-changing positions, and it is this incredible endurance that gives the book an almost tragic shine.

Indeed, Karatani's decade-long struggle cannot be adequately described in terms of the autonomous performance of text as such, but more as relentless waves of battle that record their own strategic displacements and weave themselves into a production. Karatani himself has spoken about the nature of his approach during this period:

I deliberately attempted to entrap myself "within." In this process, I strictly forbade myself to assume either of two attitudes: on one hand, I determined not to presuppose exteriority as something that exists substantively, because exteriority, once grasped as such, is already internal. . . . At the same time I decided not to deal with this issue "poetically," because it is the last possible recourse—a common and indulgent trick. I tried to speak as rigorously as I could in order to block every possible way of sneaking out of formalization.

This double-bind caused me a great deal of difficulty; however, I voluntarily chose this severely restricted and minimalist path in order to give the coup de grâce to ambiguous and inconsistent discourses once and for all. Consequently, at least I can now acknowledge to myself that I have done everything possible by methods that were initiated by "introspection." *Language, Number, Money* was supposed to encompass all my attempts of the previous decade, but the crisis this produced was so serious—it struck me so severely, both mentally and physically—that I had to give it up.

Indicated as it is in the subtitle for the present book, something radical of "Language, Number, Money" is inscribed herein. Indeed, the book absorbs some aspects of all the aforementioned essays: parts one and two correspond to the works previous to "Researches," and part three embodies some aspects of *Researches I*.

By Karatani's own admission, "Researches" marked a decisive turn. It functions as a fundamental critique of his previous work. Nevertheless, it should not be seen as something conclusive, because in a sense it is a reexamination of the views that were already presented, albeit rather more intuitively, in the first work of the group, *Marx: The Center of His Possibilities*. In this sense, notions of "development" or "synthesis" might not elucidate the actual intertextual movements that occur.

Finally, in a number of ways, this edition is a totally new book that has its own peculiar integrity, independent of any of the above, and it is unique in that it bridges the work prior to and including "Researches."

Karatani's Critique

Ever since he published his first work in 1969 at the age of 27, Karatani has operated in a domain that can provisionally be called "criticism." In Japan he is known as a literary critic, and with the publication in English of *Origins of Modern Japanese Literature* (Duke University Press, 1993), he has been officially introduced as a scholar of literature in the American context. However, as one might notice in his approach in *Origins*, "literature" (*bungaku*) for Karatani amounts to the critique of the philosophical problematics that reside at the core of discursive events; his role in Japan's contemporary intellectual scene in fact extends beyond the literary circle. He calls himself a critic—but not in the sense of one who judges the value of *oeuvres* in a specific genre; it is more as an independent critical mind that engages "transcendentally" in the mechanisms of discursive historicity, penetrating a multitude of domains. Karatani's approach corresponds to Paul de Man's "language-centered" assessment of philosophy in its concentrated formalization, yet he also persists in the will to expand the critique of formalization to the larger power field (of *discours*) to detect the omnipresent nexus of architecture as a metaphor.

In the introduction to this book, Arata Isozaki mentions Karatani's idiosyncratic tendency to traverse various academic genres: "He transgresses categories by using his questioning to dig vertically through each domain while at the same time remaining within it." The fragmentary nature of this book is attributable to this approach: each chapter deals with a different disciplinary framework, yet separately and together they are all devised to detect the mechanism of the metaphor. Karatani's voice refuses to be directed toward and consumed by a circle of specialists. In his practice the identity of the intended reader is itself questioned and radically dislodged as he attempts to undo the entrapping mechanisms of the normative coding that fosters an enclosed communality where voices tend to be absorbed into the homogeneous black hole. This distantiation of his voice might not have come about so deliberately if it had been totally detached from the geopolitical conditions emphatically witnessed in Japan, yet it is clear that his work cannot be illuminated merely by scrutinizing its "Japan-ness" either.

Rather than constructing an alternative "community" model for a better future as such, Karatani's tactic is to concentrate on the critical practices that attempt to reveal what one might call a bare eventuality in the "social" problematics, which—though repressed within the inversive nature of discourse—can never be dissolved or sublated. Rather, it is this very eventuality, which is omitted from the foundation of knowledge, that forms the most ubiquitous condition of our communication; it is something that we live with (though without being aware of) and hence cannot touch upon; it is an absolute exteriority that nevertheless binds our mode of existence (from within). Karatani's work unfolds—though only for an instant as sharp and intense as a lightning strike—the possibility of a consciousness of this impossible mechanism that constantly swerves away from ideational and structural encoding.

Karatani approaches the aporia in the entangled rapport between the eventuality and the becoming of our discourses in a number of ways. His analytical procedure somewhat approximates the Nietzschean genealogy that reveals the perversity inherent in causality, but the idiosyncrasy of Karatani's "genealogy" lies in its trajectory along the phenomenological critique of *Inexistenz*. Inasmuch as any cognitive process actually begins with (and proceeds along with) our consciousness, regardless of whether in the end the consciousness discovers itself as an effect or an agent for something else, the analysis has no other choice than to be primarily "introspective." Karatani's methodology of "genealogical retrospection" thus persists in proceeding by way of introspection in a Husserlian manner rather than directly approaching its objects, for example "discourses" or "archives."

Karatani has discussed the intricate reciprocity between introspective and retrospective drives in the actual critical practices of Nietzsche and Husserl. These passages are taken from the author's foreword to *Introspection and Retrospection* (1980):

In *The Will to Power*, Nietzsche stresses the danger of the consciousness directly questioning consciousness and cautions us rather to question "the body and physiology as the starting point." Yet the purport of his method is not to explicate the becoming of consciousness by means of the external fact of consciousness, for such an external and objective fact is not the cause, but rather something that is discovered as an effect of consciousness itself; in other words, this notion of external and objective fact has already been netted by "consciousness." Instead of directly questioning consciousness, Nietzsche's "questioning the body" amounts to nothing more than a tactic of continually making a detour around the "danger" of "direct questioning of the subject about subject," yet at the same time it does just that. Indeed, what is of crucial importance here is not what Nietzsche illuminated with his question but rather the way he questions, or the nature of the problematic that makes this manner of questioning inevitable. His retrospective queries might be called philology or genealogy, though they are far from philology or genealogy as commonly understood. In Nietzsche, retrospection is never done along the external factuality—biological, physical, historical; it can be done only within introspection and, at the same time, as a rejection of introspection.

Husserlian phenomenology is the most sophisticated and extreme form of "consciousness directly questioning consciousness"; nevertheless it is not exempted from the "danger" that Nietzsche points out, because Husserl's introspective retrospection that persisted up to the advent of body could never be extricated from its teleological framework. The retrospection in Nietzsche is, on the one hand, a phenomenological retrospection, and, on the other, exists as something that reverses each teleological posture inherent in the retrospection, one by one. Nietzsche's proposition of "questioning the body" must be seen as such. The word "questioning" implies that it is an introspective/reductive query; simultaneously, though, it must be noted that what is "questioned" is not the "consciousness" but the "body." "Body" in this context is not that which is yielded as an end result of the phenomenological reduction, but, conversely, that which rejects the introspective evidence within the reduction. Therefore, the phrase "questioning the body" is a metaphor. It is simultaneously both a phenomenological retrospection and the disorganization of the teleological conformity that enables such retrospection.

What is more, Karatani's reading of Marx has a great deal to do with this analytical procedure:

Marx's so-called "dialectics" in *Capital* exists in its peculiar description that retrospectively reveals the inversion—fabrication of necessity out of contingency—entailed in Hegelian categorizations; it detects this mechanism, case by case, one by one, whenever a becoming of a category occurs, all the while following the line of Hegelian thought. In other words, the dynamics of *Capital* is that it constructs problematics in the mode of Hegel and at the same time deconstructs them, since there is indeed no other possibility of executing a "critique" of Hegel.

In Karatani's epistemology, Marx's engagement in the field of Hegelian construction corresponds to the way Nietzsche's "genealogy" can be applied to Husserlian introspection: both Nietzsche and Marx are seen as critiques—Marx to Hegelian phenomenology and Nietzsche to Husserlian phenomenology. Thus Karatani's genealogy can be seen as Marxian as well as Nietzschean. The formalization (introspection) and its critique, if seen from the macro level, are actually links in a chain of events between his sequential approaches, as we have seen in the relationship of his works pre- and post-"Researches." This English edition of *Architecture as Metaphor* thus shares the structure that "formalization" precedes (parts one and two), and meta-critique follows (part three).

On Karatani's Singularity

One of the terms that stands out in part three is *tandokusei*—"singularity." *Researches II* (1989) opens with an essay entitled "Singularity and Particularity," in which Karatani begins his demonstration with a personal recollection:

Ever since I started reading philosophy in my teens, I always have felt that "this I" was missing in what I read. Regardless of the way it is presented—subject, existence, human being, and the like—philosophical discourses invariably deal with the "I" in general terms. The "I" is nothing other than something attributable to the millions of persons to which "this I" does not belong. Therein lies the reason for my never being able to familiarize myself with philosophy, and why I always felt alienated from it.

However, my concern was not about "me" and it does not imply that "this I" is special. I am not special. I know how common I am and yet "this I" feels "am not anyone else."

What is at stake here is the "this" in "this I" and not the consciousness, I. Therefore, instead of saying that "this I" has been omitted from the philosophical discourse, one could put it in another way; that "this thing" has been omitted from the philosophical discourse. For instance, when I say "this dog," it does not indicate a particular one among the genus *Canis* (in general). The "this"-ness of this dog named Taro has nothing to do with its features and characteristics. It is simply "this dog."

I will call the "this"-ness of "this I" or "this dog" *singularity*, to distinguish it from *particularity*. *Singularity*, as explained later, does not mean that a thing is only one. Singularity, as opposed to particularity—that is, an individuality seen from a position of generality—is an individuality no longer able to belong to the realm of generality. We must distinguish (1) "I am" from (2) "this I am": the "I" in (1) is one (a particular) of the I's in general, pertinent to any one of the I's, but the "I" in (2) is *singular*, irreplaceable by any other I. Of course, it does not mean in the least that "this I" is too special to be replaced. Therefore, "this I" or "this dog," even without any special characteristics, is still *singular*.

There is no doubt that Karatani persists in the existentialist problematization of singularity in the vein of Max Stirner and Søren Kierkegaard; at the same time, however, his course of pursuit is distanced from their "introspection" by means of the inversion. First, his discussion takes a cue from "singularity" in the mathematical sense—the point that cannot be differentiated; in Leibnizian monadology/differentiation, when an individual expresses generality, singularity implies "this individuality" in the individual as disconnected from generality; in other words, this point (monad) is singular, rather than particular. "This" as singularity is not a simple demonstrative, but actually indicates "none-other-than-this"—meaning that "it happens to be this way, though it could have been other ways." At this point, the theory of modality (possible worlds) must be introduced, for it is in such a context that Karatani treats singularity as the problematic of proper names, somewhat as Saul Kripke does. He stresses that the singularity that is distinct from particularity is inseparable from the proper name.

What must be noted, however, is the complexity of the procedure he uses to deal with the singularity problem: on the one hand, he shifts the existentialist discussion of singularity to the problematic of the proper name; on the other, he further attempts to reintroduce the existentialist problematic into the discussion of proper name. It is clearly by way of this maneuver that his term "social" appears with its twofold connotation that must be understood as distinct from Kripke's notion of precedence of community. Karatani's "sociality" apparently subsumes the Kierkegaardian "leap." Or, it is Karatani who reads the Marxian "social" with a nuance that exposes its uncontrollable eventuality.

Therefore, even though he was inspired by these ideas of singularity and also by those of Gilles Deleuze, his position diverges from those of Western philosophers in its unique materialism that grasps singularity as an eventuality of the proper name that can never be internalized within any monistic concept. Instead of positing it in a realm totally separate and opposite from the "social"—rather than including it in the idealist common essence or the existentialist subject—he stresses that it is this singularity that reveals "sociality." As discussed in the book, classical economics finds the "common essence" (objectified labor-time) within every commodity/individual, and therefore each individual is treated as the particularized general; it follows that the "crisis" inherent in exchange is ignored, or rather, the

exchange as an event is itself omitted. In actuality, however, two different commodities are deemed to share a
"common essence" simply as a result of the event of
exchange (equation) that has factually occurred; classical
economics confuses the effect with the cause inversely. It
is in response to this point that Karatani interjects
"Marxian genealogy." To paraphrase Karatani, what
Marx called "social" is the exchange/communication as a
"fatal leap (*salto mortale*)" that cannot presuppose communality, and this sociality is inseparable from the fact
that each commodity or individual is in essence a singular existence that is by no means ascribable to generality.

Karatani extracts the eventuality of a number of
forms in various discursive contexts in order to shed
light on this blank—the non-knowledge—in our social
practices/speculations; it can never be coherently
described, but only expressed ultimately in the form of a
risk, a bet, or a leap; otherwise, it will only be fictively
constructed *ex post facto*. Karatani's stance toward "this"
is projected, most crucially, as a critique of metaphysics.
He calls this position "philosophy of speculation," if not
speculative philosophy.

In part three, terms such as "community," "society,"
and "intercrossing space (*Verkehrsraum*)" stand out.
These concepts are inseparable from the aforementioned "sociality": as opposed to a communal space
where common rules for exchange are shared, in the
social space "in between" communities no common rules
can be presupposed in principle. What is more, as
Karatani stresses, in our ordinary situations it is fundamental rather than anomalous to form the "secular
tragedy." Therefore, in the manner of the "genealogical
retrospection" or "Marxian genealogy," Karatani reverses the order of the sociological method, which generally
starts from the community model and then discusses the

relation with the exterior afterward. He goes on to say that individual communities are just like islands that float on the ocean of intercrossing space. The paragraph that follows tells how the social, intercrossing space can be hypothetically extracted; it is quoted from *Researches II*.

Our hypothesis would first suppose an "intercrossing space" that completely lacks the division of interior and exterior, and then consider that communities formed their "interiors" as if each of them folded themselves inwardly here and there on the otherwise indivisible space. This space has existed since the pre-community stage and persists to this day; at present, mediated by money, it forms a network of global relations that are incessantly organized, disorganized, and reorganized. This "intercrossing space" is a transnational movement that individual communities (nation-states) can by no means partition; even though every single community is totally dependent on the space, it never gives up its obsessive attempt to segregate itself in order to sustain the identity of its own "interiority."

Soon after this passage, the author stresses a way to define the "community" so that it can be amplified to include any space that produces and sustains "interiority" and "exteriority." Indeed, this mechanism can be observed in a number of senses in various entities from the nation-state to the individual.

A Few Issues Concerning the Translation

The translation of Japanese contemporary theory into English inexorably involves some complications due to the peculiar position of Japanese vis-à-vis Western languages. When, for instance, the German noun that Marx used—*Naturwüchsigkeit*—is translated into English, it is most often as "spontaneous." In German, however, *Spontaneität* also exists—Rosa Luxemburg used it to oppose Leninist centralism. It must be noted that Marx deliberately applied *Naturwüchsigkeit* to avoid the deistic (predetermined harmonious) nuances *Spontaneität* implies. On the other hand, *Naturwüchsigkeit* is sometimes translated as "naturally grown" or "grown naturally"; neither sustains the noun form as in the German original. This does not seem to be caused so much by a projection of the translators' intention as by a predetermination of the structure of the English language. In contrast, the Japanese translation of the term—*shizen-seicho-sei*—sustains the form of a noun, which more closely corresponds to the German original both literally and structurally. Despite the closer kinship between English and German, Japanese and German share the aspect that a neologism can be produced rather freely by compounding morphemes. In the context of Karatani's reading of Marx, this conceptualization of *Naturwüchsigkeit* as one word is crucial; therefore I kept the German term except in the first appearance where "grown-by-nature-ness" is used.

For Karatani's reading of Marx, the first edition of *Capital* is indispensable. The author pays utmost attention to an expression found only in this particular version that implies the same sort of paradox as the one that accompanies the necessary collapse of Russellian logical typing. It could be said that it was Karatani, together with the economist Katsuhito Iwai, who discovered this correspondence between Marxian and mathematical problematics. This reading of Marx had an enormous impact on the Japanese intellectual scene in the early 1980s. The existence of the English translation of this particular version of *Capital* was pointed out to me by Mr. Iwai (it is found in *Values: Studies by Marx*, edited by A. Dragstead, New Park Publications, London, 1976); in any event, it seems that there have not been discussions exclusively on this particular *lecture* of Marx in the American context.

The transcoding of concepts/translation of texts—as exemplified in *Naturwüchsigkeit*, for instance—whether directed from Europe to Japan or to the United States, has different impacts and results according to each context. Now, in the course of the translation of a book such as this, not only the book itself but also these different metamorphoses of European concepts—the subconscious of the book—have began to crash over the Pacific Ocean, as if closing the cycle that started in Europe and then split toward the East and West.

As a response to the long history of exportation of intellectual products from Europe and America to Japan, the new lines of intercourse yet to be developed and challenged—especially in the realm of theoretical works—are those from Japan, and more widely from the Far East. In contrast, the situation between Europe and America, spanning the Atlantic Ocean, has been slightly different: mutual intellectual exchanges have already been active among English-language, German, and French philosophies. John Rajchman described the exchange that occurred during the 1980s over the Atlantic Ocean in terms of a "translation without a master," where, unlike in the conventional situation of translation, we can no longer assume a basis provided by a voice of a master on either side (translating or translated) that regulates the canonical measure to judge the final destination of what is translated. He describes its characteristics:

This lack of mastery, this freedom might be contrasted with, and used to analyze, two other situations or images of translation: that of *fidelity*, where the other is the master and the problem is one of identification with his words; and that of *charity*, where one can't help being oneself the master, and the problem is the altruistic one of knowing what should be, or should have been, good or true for the other. For it is the freedom of translation that allows us to discern the obsessional side of fidelity (no other set of words can ever be adequate to that of the master) and the autistic side of charity (nothing in the words of the other can alter the basic representations one used to identify oneself). Conversely, translation without a master would be the art of breaking with those with whom one nevertheless identifies, while exposing oneself to the singularities of those one nevertheless tries to understand.

The "translation without a master"—this radically new condition of exchange—is reminiscent of the "asymmetric relation" inherent in the "teaching-learning" and "selling-buying" relations that Karatani detects in our basic social conditions, in the sense that no common basis can be presupposed and no neutral/transcendent position in between can substantively exist; it is where the *salto mortale* must absolutely be confronted. And yet, at the same time, to face such a situation as it is, consciously and strategically, might amount to the "freedom" that John Rajchman defines.

In a number of senses, this translation itself has been an illustration of the aporia that Karatani challenges in this book. Strangely enough, it is "self-referential" in that the pivotal problematics within communication that weave some, if not all, aspects of the book have been substantially involved in the process of translation: it is a *salto mortale* for the translator, who—in a transgression of the canon of translation—translated from his mother tongue (Japanese) to an "other" tongue (English), and at the same time it is an unpredictable exchange within the intercrossing space—beyond the border of communities—in which no outcome can be predicted.

Karatani has spoken of the notion of "infinity" that was achieved paradoxically at the moment that the worldview was closed:

Descartes conceived of universal spaces that are divided into interior and exterior. This space is an infinite extension, but for Descartes this infinity is a notion derived from the negation of the finite. In contrast, Spinoza grasped the infinite positively. He looked upon the world itself as the infinite, meaning actually that the world is closed, that there is nothing beyond this world (= God = nature), and that even the transcendental God is no more than an imaginary product from within this world.

And, by connecting Spinoza to non-Euclidean geometry, where the Euclidean plane is metamorphosed into a sphere, and to Giordano Bruno, who relativized the notion of the globe vis-à-vis other planets, Karatani makes us think of this act of closing the world in different discursive realms—and it makes me think especially of the possibility of the transcoding/translation around the full globe that is yet to be seen; between the Far East and America in particular. To be sure, this closing does not mean that the world will be unified into a homogeneous system; on the contrary, it will reveal more heterogeneity and more confrontations between the differences. Therefore it is necessary to share "the map of crises" not in a pessimistic sense but in a critical one. In terms both of its content and situation, namely as an event in a full sense, *Architecture as Metaphor* marks the advent of the "translation without a master" over the Pacific Ocean.

Sabu Kohso

Since 1970, many things have been claimed in the name of deconstruction. In the following chapters I examine the problematic of deconstruction from the standpoint of construction, that is, from the standpoint of architecture. It is now clear that many post-sixties architects worked parallel to, and in some cases even precursory to and therefore independent of, the various deconstructions being developed in philosophy and literary criticism. Postmodernism, understood as an idea or concept that includes deconstruction and the other discourses of poststructuralism, might be said to have originated precisely in architecture. It is also clear that structure, likewise understood as a concept, is architectural; indeed, architectural metaphors have been widely used in the various discourses of structuralism and poststructuralism.

In his attempt to define the philosopher, Plato employed the architect as a metaphor. For Plato, architecture meant, more than anything else, an active position that enables one to resist or withstand all "becomings" by reconstructing them as "makings": "By its original meaning [*poiesis*] means simply creation, and creation, as you know, can take very various forms. Any action which is the cause of a thing emerging from non-existence into existence might be called [*poiesis*], and all the processes in all the crafts are kinds of [*poiesis*], and all those who are engaged in them [creators]."[1] Plato likened philosophers who took such a position to architects. Yet like other Athenians of his time, Plato despised the manual labor involved in building. Unlike the substantial materiality of architecture, which belongs to the realm of what we might call "semi-becoming," Platonic architecture is metaphorical. Plato's use of the metaphor of architecture, like that of Descartes, Kant, and Hegel who followed him, should thus be understood as the will to construct an edifice of knowledge on a solid foundation.

Plato consistently embraced geometry as a norm, but because he overlooked the algebraic systems that had been developed in Babylonia, his contribution to mathematics amounted to little in a practical sense. Instead, Plato recast both algebra and geometry in the form of a solid edifice, an architectonic. Even though, like architecture, mathematics is semi-becoming, philosophers since Plato have turned to mathematics because it ostensibly offers the ideal ground or architectonic on which something genuinely new can be established. Philosophy, in fact, is another name for this *will to architecture*. Architecture as a metaphor dominated mathematics and even architecture itself until 1931, when Kurt Gödel's incompleteness theorem invalidated mathematics as the ground for the architectonic.

In the 1970s the "text" replaced architecture as the dominant metaphor or figure. Roland Barthes distinguished the text from the work, arguing that the work is a self-contained whole dependent on the author for its meaning or signification, while the text is a textured fabric of quotations and metonymical slidings that produces significations without recourse to the sovereign author. But Barthes and the various practices of literary criticism were not the only pioneers in the development of textuality. Parallel strategies were emerging in many disciplines. For example, the anthropologist Claude Lévi-Strauss opposed the concept of *bricolage* to making. And in architecture, the text—even if not named as such—was, by this time, already supplanting architecture as the dominant metaphor. It is this trend that we now call postmodernism. This shift from architecture to text as privileged metaphor favors becoming over making, and continues in the tradition of thinkers such as Hume (as opposed to Kant), and Montaigne (as opposed to Descartes) who affirm textual manifoldness. Reconsidering this shift ultimately returns us to Plato.

Despite my own sympathies with the shift from architecture to text, I had many reservations. I wrote the first part of the present book when I was teaching at Yale University in 1980, at a time when I was reexamining the poststructuralist problematic. In the North American context, poststructuralism appeared to me too closely connected to literary criticism. For example, that one of Jacques Derrida's early works was an annotation to Husserl's *The Origin of Geometry*, and not an analysis of literature, was almost completely overlooked.[2] It seemed to me that even Derrida himself was too strictly conforming his work to North American literary criticism. Though I am a literary critic, I wanted, at that time, to protest against such a supraliterary tendency. I wanted to insist that deconstruction could be realized only by exhaustive construction; otherwise, it would degenerate into mere word games.

Plato did attack poets. The poetic counterattacks against Plato that were initiated in nineteenth-century romanticism were later developed and extended by Nietzsche and were again extended in the ascension of textualism to the status of privileged metaphor. These attacks have contributed to making deconstruction so extraordinarily literary, thereby obscuring its constructive dimension. Since the literary text is ambiguous, it is easy and perhaps even indulgent to stress the undecidability of its meaning. But in mathematics, the discipline where precision and decidability are considered essential, the appearance of undecidability presents a more fundamental challenge.

It was Kurt Gödel who introduced undecidability into mathematics. From my perspective, deconstruction, if formalized, is tantamount to Gödel's proof. Yet this implies neither the dominance nor the impotence of mathematics. Gödel's proof presents us with a case wherein the attempt to *architectonize* mathematics results not in a mathematical foundation but in the impossibility of mathematical foundations. Gödel's proof of the lack of mathematical foundation is, however, emancipatory rather than restrictive for mathematics. Mathematics is a study that focuses on relation: contrary to the romanticist idea that mathematics is a study of number and quantity, mathematics scrutinizes only relation—for that matter, even number and quantity are forms of relation. But this raises the question of whether or not relation exists in the same way that material does. Plato speculated that relation exists in a different way; concurring with this, Marx noted that in language every relation is expressed only conceptually. It was perhaps inevitable, then, that many in the modern period who dealt with relation followed the idealist path—a path, it should be noted, that is not avoided simply by invoking material and perception.

Many formalists of this century, including the mathematician David Hilbert and the linguist Ferdinand de Saussure, insisted on the existence of certain ideal forms while simultaneously rejecting the notion that they exist in some real place. Formalism apprehends the form as a precedent and the object and the sense one makes of it as the model or interpretation of the form. It is not an exaggeration to say that some of the major intellectual issues of the twentieth century were provoked by the radical reversal of formalism as such. For example, both Saussure's linguistic model—which argues that the *signifier* exists only as a differential form, and that the *signified*, or meaning, is merely its product—and Lévi-Strauss's anthropological methodology—which, instead of deriving a model from empirical fact, builds the mathematical structure first and then observes empirical fact as a model that interprets the structure—are fundamentally formalist modes of thinking.

Formalism emerged in numerous fields of study: linguistics, cultural anthropology, psychoanalysis, intellectual history, and so on. However, diverse generic application did not facilitate a radical questioning of the problematics commonly attributed to formalism. Had formalism been questioned, the problem that Plato first confronted and answered—the problem of the status of form—would undoubtedly have resurfaced. Being a Platonist himself, Gödel developed an internal critique of formalism that had repercussions in formalist practices in all disciplinary fields. Plato did not capriciously pose the being of the *ideal*, or the foundation of knowledge. Indeed, he failed rather miserably in his attempt to implement his idea of the philosopher-king. Instead, Plato realized the impossible in the *imaginaire*: he made Socrates a martyr to this impossible-to-achieve idea, in the same way, for example, that St. Paul exalted Jesus. All of this demonstrates the impossibility of the *being* of the *ideal* and yet, at the same time, it repeatedly invokes the *will to architecture* by asserting that the impossible, the *being* of the *ideal*, be realized. This *will to architecture* is the foundation of Western thought.

In my own work I could not simply deny this will. My thinking developed as follows: I assumed as a premise that a consistently critical attitude would reveal its own ungroundedness and thus reveal its own becoming; only persistent formalization or construction, I realized, would lead to the exteriority of form. To critique constructionism, however, requires more than simply invoking becoming. Becoming, or, to use Marx's term, "grown-by-nature-ness" (*Naturwüchsigkeit*),[3] is not so formless or chaotic as it seems, but is rather something that can be formally demonstrated. I owe this insight to a group of city planning theorists who at the time were dealing with the problem of "natural cities." In part two of this book, I overturn the conventional conception of becoming as *Naturwüchsigkeit* and develop an account of it as a self-referential formal system. Language is not simply a differential system but a self-referential differential system, and by extension, as we will see in the concluding chapters of this book, the currency or monetary economy is a self-referential system of commodities.

It was at this point that my original project was interrupted; if it were granted that becoming itself could be formalized, the exterior of the formal system would have to be regarded as nonexistent. In the course of my attempt to move out of or beyond the formal system by a process of persistent formalization, I found myself trapped within a new type of enclosure, where—worse still—I could no longer even assume an exterior. My predicament at the time notwithstanding, we can now see that though the monetary economy appears as a self-referential formal system of commodities, in reality there undoubtedly exists somewhere (in some monetary or economic realm) an exterior; the general equivalent—money—is guaranteed only by the presupposition that money is able at any time to return to the form of commodity, as in the case of gold. This is where the market's so-called auto-adjustment mechanism, which Adam Smith referred to as the "invisible hand," enters the picture. This same invisible mechanism has more recently been called "spontaneous order" and "self-organizing system."

The exteriority of money vis-à-vis the commodity, however, can never be interiorized or brought into the relational commodity system: no matter how high the price of gold, money cannot be metamorphosed into gold because this conversion—transforming gold into money and money into gold—is inevitably accompanied by a loss in weight. Moreover, gold is money only because it is expressed in the money form; it is only a convention. A piece of paper can be money, for example, if it is expressed in the money form. What Marx demonstrated in his theory of the money form was that the relationship between money and commodity can be explained only through the development of an asymmetrical system of forms—the relative value form and the equivalent form. That is to say, the asymmetry in the relation between money and commodity—or, more precisely, between buying and selling—has existed primordially and can never be overcome. Herein lies the crisis that Marx often refers to.

I nevertheless found it impossible to reintroduce such an exteriority in my work by following the preexisting line of formalization. A more decisive "turn" was required. Consequently, I abandoned the Japanese edition of *Architecture as Metaphor* and the subsequent work *Language, Number, Money* halfway through. In this state of stagnation, trapped in a cul-de-sac, what struck me quite forcefully was Edward Said's book *The World, the Text, and the Critic*, in particular the essay entitled "Secular Criticism."

And yet something happened, perhaps inevitably. From being a bold interventionary movement across lines of specialization, American literary theory of the late seventies had retreated into the labyrinth of "textuality," dragging along with it the most recent apostles of European revolutionary textuality—Derrida and Foucault—whose trans-Atlantic canonization and domestication they themselves seemed sadly enough to be encouraging. It is not too much to say that American or even European literary theory now explicitly accepts the principle of noninterference, and that its peculiar mode of appropriating its subject matter (to use Althusser's formula) is *not* to appropriate anything that is worldly, circumstantial, or socially contaminated. "Textuality" is the somewhat mystical and disinfected subject matter of literary theory.

Textuality has therefore become the exact antithesis and displacement of what might be called history. Textuality is considered to take place, yes, but by the same token it does not take place anywhere or anytime in particular. It is produced, but by no one and at no time. . . . As it is practiced in the American academy today, literary theory has for the most part isolated textuality from the circumstances, the events, the physical senses that made it possible and render it intelligible as the result of human work.

My position is that texts are worldly, to some degree they are events, and even when they appear to deny it, they are nevertheless a part of the social world, human life, and of course the historical moments in which they are located and interpreted.[4]

Said's remarks appeared to me focused precisely on the situation in which I found myself trapped. However, for me, secular criticism had to be developed within the context of my own work. In those days I was reencountering the work of Ludwig Wittgenstein, specifically his thesis on mathematical foundations. Wittgenstein argued that mathematics is a motley bundle of diverse inventions that cannot be unified into a single or unitary foundation. Mathematics is a product of historical practices. Though this sounds similar to the notion of text as a metaphor, it is completely different. If we take into account the preeminently constructive tendency of Wittgenstein's early pursuits, this "turn" is not insignificant. Far from being ignorant of Gödel's approach, Wittgenstein was completely aware of it, as evidenced by his statement "It is my task, not to attack Russell's logic from within, but from without."[5] But Wittgenstein did not follow the same path as Gödel. From Wittgenstein's point of view, Gödel had no choice but to remain "within" Russell's conceptual framework. How, then, could the "without" be possible? Only, I determined, by way of "secular criticism."

Nothing is less relevant to the reality of architecture than the idea that it is the realization of a design *qua* idea. Far more critical factors are involved, such as the collaboration with other staff members and the dialogue with and persuasion of the client. The design, as initially conceived, is invariably destined to be transformed during the course of its execution. Design is similar to Wittgenstein's term "game," where, as he says, "we play and—make up the rules as we go along."[6] No architect can predict the result. No architecture is free of its context. Architecture is an event par excellence in the sense that it is a making or a becoming that exceeds the maker's control.

Plato admired the architect as a metaphor but despised the architect as an earthly laborer, because the actual architect, and even architecture itself, are exposed to contingency. Contingency does not imply, however, that, as opposed to the designer's ideal, the actual architecture is secondary and constantly in danger of collapse. Rather, contingency insures that no architect is able to determine a design free from the relationship with the "other"—the client, staff, and other factors relevant to the design process. All architects face this other. Architecture is thus a form of communication conditioned to occur without common rules—it is a communication with the other, who, by definition, does not follow the same set of rules.

Because architecture is an event, it is always contingent. To invoke the poet, or the literary, in an attempt to refute Plato's philosophical, architectonic use of the architect as metaphor leads only to another sanctification. In order to move beyond architecture as a metaphor, the most pedestrian understanding of architecture must be used as a metaphor. In that way, the most "secular" conditions inherent in architecture can be considered. Since Plato's intervention, architecture as a metaphor has not suppressed becoming or text, but it has suppressed the "secular architect." Thus it is not the "absolute other" but the "secular other" who is able to deconstruct the self-sufficient formal system based on architecture as a metaphor. In part three of this book (a version of a series of essays entitled "Researches" that I started after the interruption of the original *Architecture as Metaphor*), I examine Wittgenstein and Marx from this new position or perspective of secular criticism. Part three, in particular, is meant to form a secular criticism to parts one and two.

Looking back now at my previous work, I am beginning to understand two things. First, I might have been unwittingly engaging in a kind of Kantian critique all along. My works have been interventions that critically examine architecture as metaphor in order to expose its limits. The target I had in mind at the outset of the present work was the dominant ideology of modernism, understood as the "grand narrative" that insists on "constructing" human society. I became aware of Kant only after "architecture as metaphor" collapsed; at that point it became evident to me that far from creating a total disappearance of the grand narrative, this collapse produced instead a set of alternative narratives or ideologies, namely the "end of history" debate (the ultimate assertion of the superiority of Western reason) and cynicism. "Architecture as metaphor" cannot be dissolved by denial. Today it is the Kantian transcendental critique that is called for. And it is in light of these considerations that I have begun to reevaluate my previous work.

Kant maintained that while logic is an analytic judgment, mathematics is an a priori synthetic judgment; mathematics requires sensuous intuition and thus cannot be logically grounded. In fact, it is precisely because it cannot be grounded that mathematics is an open-ended mode of inquiry. (This account of mathematics as a synthetic judgment was nevertheless scornfully denounced by post-Kantian philosophers.) Gottlob Frege's and Bertrand Russell's treatment of mathematics as subordinate to logic became conventional in the study of mathematical foundations. It was Gödel who criticized this convention by invoking the Kantian antinomy—undecidability—and it was Wittgenstein who criticized it from the orientation of practical ethics. This does not mean, however, that post-Kantian philosophy has been a series of hapless struggles. Instead it is only in the ruins of those struggles that for the first time we can begin to excavate the possibilities embedded in Kant. In this way, Kant's role can be extended and amplified on many different levels.

Kant called that which is constituted by the form of subjectivity "phenomenon" and that which affects subjectivity, yet cannot be composed by it, the "thing-in-itself." The thing-in-itself can be conceptualized, though it cannot be experienced. It follows that our recognition can only be synthetic judgment. In this way, Kant came to regard those thoughts that theoretically grasp the thing-in-itself as an "arrogation of reason." Kant called these thoughts *Schein* (semblance): what is understood by the term *Idee* (idea) is a *Schein*. Kant's thing-in-itself is neither the *Hinterwelt* nor the true world, but the opposite; he means to criticize such realms by suggesting that they are mere *Schein*. At the same time, Kant did not simply dismiss *Idee*; instead, he asserted that *Idee* cannot be proven theoretically, and therefore must not be realized constitutively. Even so, *Schein* is indispensable in that it functions regulatively. In this way, the triad of thing-in-itself, phenomenon, and *Schein* constitute a structure whose potential is fundamentally compromised if even one of the three is discarded.[7]

The antiquated term "thing-in-itself," for example, can be discarded and replaced with something else if we wish, but the composition of the triadic structure cannot. In psychoanalysis, Lacan's categories "Real," "Symbolic," and "Imaginary" are similar to the Kantian divisions thing-in-itself, phenomenon, and *Idee*. Freudian psychoanalysis was established as a metapsychology, as a transcendental psychology; as post-Freudian psychoanalysis degenerated into an empirical psychology, Lacan appeared on the scene to revive the "transcendental critique." Lacan became aware of Kant, however, long after the invention of his own triadic formula. Many thinkers who appear to be antagonistic toward Kant—Marx and Nietzsche, for example—reprised, employing different terms, the same structure that Kant introduced. In other words, these thinkers attempted to revive the thing-in-itself on their own terms and in different contexts. As I have sought to argue in what follows, Marx presented a historicity to which we belong and by which we are constantly motivated, a historicity that, paradoxically, slips through the framing of any construction built with linguistic speculation. This historicity is, in other words, a *naturwüchsiges* manifold. Furthermore, Marx's *Capital*, as its subtitle, "The Critique of Political Economy," implies, is neither a denial nor an affirmation of classical economics or of Hegel, but a Kantian "critique" of them. What Marx attempted, then, was a transcendental rather than an empirical retrospection of the value form.

The fact that Kant's triadic concept is replaceable with different triads indicates that it forms a kind of structure that can be grasped transcendentally. Kant called this structure "architectonics." While philosophical discourses generally disregard rhetoric in order to achieve their much-desired precision, and philosophers, especially those who emerged after Kant, sought to do away with figurative expression, Kant's critique is marked by the omnipresence of the "metaphor." Kant employed architectonics as a metaphor in the following way:

For if such a system is some day worked out under the general name of Metaphysic—and its full and complete execution is both possible and of the utmost importance for the employment of reason in all departments of its activity—the critical examination of the ground for this edifice must have been previously carried down to the very depths of the foundations of the faculty of principles independent of experience, lest in some quarter it might give way, and, sinking, inevitably bring with it the ruin of all.[8]

Although at first glance Kant appears to incline toward the Platonic use of architecture as metaphor, the opposite is true. Kant claimed in the *Critique of Pure Reason* that his investigation could not properly be called a doctrine, but should instead be called transcendental critique. To put it differently, Kant's critiques were intended not to construct a system but to reveal that any system "inevitably bring[s] with it the ruin of all" inasmuch as it is upheld under the aegis of the "arrogation of reason." Since "arrogation" is a juridical term, Kant's architectonics might also be substituted by a set of juridical metaphors. What is crucial to note is that architectonics as metaphor is indispensable to the critique of architecture as metaphor.

What Kant called the "Copernican turn" offered a position from which to consider the world that humans recognize as a "phenomenon"; it implied a view from which to see the world not as a copy of something that exists externally, but as that which is only constituted by "throwing in" a certain form or category. It is possible to see twentieth-century formalism, including the linguistic turn, as an expansion of the Kantian inversion. Yet to stop there ignores Kant's pivotal role. The "Copernican turn" literally reverses the man/earth-centered view in favor of a heliocentric view; Kant's turn, metaphorically speaking, is a turn toward the "thing-in-itself"/heliocentric position. Because of its inherent lack of the thing-in-itself, formalism, understood in the broadest sense, inevitably leads to a humanism of another kind, to textual idealism, or to skepticism. The "turns" that I analyze apropos Marx and Wittgenstein are the ones that truly deserve to be called "Copernican," because from a secular perspective the thing-in-itself is the "other." Because the Kantian problematic became apparent to me only recently—after this present work was completed and thus after the historic fall of the grand narratives—I deal with it here only in notes at the end of certain chapters.

The other thing that has become clear to me concerns the reason for my turn to the issues of formalization in the first place. As a non-Westerner and foreigner, I could not, nor did I need to, participate in the wordplay that, at the time, was a requisite of Western theoretical writing. Despite, or rather because of, the fact that I am a literary critic myself, I deliberately swerved away from literature. In the cultural soil of Japan, no critical impact could be achieved from such a stratagem carried out *à la lettre*: in Japan, the will to architecture does not exist—a circumstance that allowed postmodernism to blossom in its own way. Unlike in the West, deconstructive forces are constantly at work in Japan. As strange as it may sound, being architectonic in Japan is actually radical and political. Therefore I had to act like a performer with dual roles: at the same time that I was investigating the perverted origin of the will to architecture, I had to analyze the origin of the deconstructive power structure that suffuses Japan.

As I mentioned earlier, an overwhelming feeling of emptiness and futility interrupted me in the midst of my pursuit, which was due, I now assume, not only to the self-referential nature of my investigation but also to my required performance of dual roles. Although in this book I have not mentioned my Japanese predecessors in these struggles, I am a beneficiary of their intellectual legacy and more than conscious of their importance. Among them, I would especially like to name an architect, Arata Isozaki. It was his book *The Dissolution of Architecture* (1975) that prompted me to speculate on deconstruction through the problematics of construction. Regardless of Isozaki's reception abroad, he was at that time the only architect in Japan who dared to confront head-on the issues of modernity. Isozaki, too, was living dual roles: while criticizing Japanese modernity and architecture he persisted in the will to architecture. Moreover, it was Isozaki who, to my surprise, most highly appreciated the importance of *Architecture as Metaphor*, which had not been directed toward architects and has but little relevance to architecture in a narrow sense. Thus my primary gratitude goes to him. I would also like to thank the American architect Peter Eisenman and the editor-in-chief of Anyone Corporation, Cynthia Davidson, who heard of this work from Isozaki and determined to publish it in America.

This book is not aimed at architects in a narrow sense. I would be honored, however, if it were read by those who, though denying architecture with a capital A, strive to be architectonic, and those who, denying subject with a capital S, choose to be subjects of and as difference.

Finally, I thank Sabu Kohso and Judy Geib for their translation and Michael Speaks for his editorial work. It was the passion and zeal of these three that encouraged me to face this work that I otherwise would have allowed to rest in peace.

Kojin Karatani
Ithaca, New York, April 1992

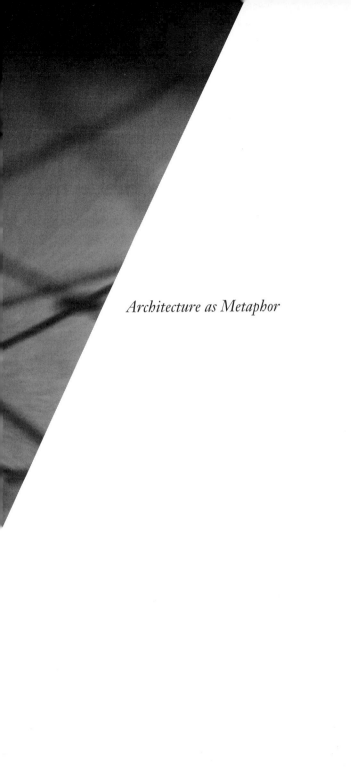

Architecture as Metaphor

Part One Making

Philosophers since Plato have returned over and
again to architectural figures and metaphors as a
way of grounding and stabilizing their otherwise
unstable philosophical systems. Descartes developed the metaphor of the city planner as a
model for producing a solid edifice of
thought, while Hegel believed that knowledge must be systematic, architectonic.
Even Kierkegaard, despite his parable
ridiculing Hegel for living in a hut
overshadowed by a magnificent edifice of Hegel's own construction,
availed himself of the metaphor   *One* **The Will to Architecture**
of architecture. Today, archi-
tectural terms are ubiquitous
in philosophical and theoretical discussions. It is
thus not coincidental that
we give the name decon-
struction to the movement
that attempts to undermine
metaphysics as it has developed
from Plato.

Western thought is marked by a
will to architecture that is reiterated
and renewed at times of crisis. The origins of this will to architecture are generally attributed to Plato. In ancient Greek,
architectonicé (architecture) is constructed from
architectonicé techné, which signifies *techné of
architectón*, *architectón* being a compound of *arché*
(origin, principle, primacy) and *tectón* (craftsman).
Among Greeks, architecture was considered not
merely a skill of craftsmen but an art practiced by those
who possess a principal knowledge and mastery of all

technologies, and who therefore plan projects and lead other craftsmen. In this context the term *techné* meant not only technology in a narrow sense but also *poiesis* (making) in general. Plato defined it in the following way: "By its original meaning [*poiesis*] means simply creation, and creation, as you know, can take very various forms. Any action which is the cause of a thing emerging from non-existence into existence might be called [*poiesis*], and all the processes in all the crafts are kinds of [*poiesis*], and all those who are engaged in them [creators]."[1] In the metaphor of architecture Plato discovered a figure that under the aegis of "making" is able to withstand "becoming."

An etymological account, however, is inadequate to explain why Plato regarded architecture as a figure of philosophy par excellence, or to explain why this figure is obsessively repeated in philosophical and theoretical discourse. Plato disdained both architecture and the real-life architect. According to F. M. Cornford, Greek thinkers can be grouped into two general types. On the one hand, evolutionists consider the world a living, growing form or organism; on the other hand, creationists consider the world a designed work of art.[2] These two types represent two worldviews: one that understands the world as becoming and another that understands the world as a product of making. The latter view was held by a minority of Greek thinkers.

This minority view required another idea to insure its existence: the notion of "God as Architect." Alfred North Whitehead argued that what sustains the sciences is neither mathematics nor certain, rigorous foundations but a faith that the world is orderly and, hence, ultimately cognizable because it is created by God the Great Architect. Whitehead claimed that this faith, which developed from Christianity and Platonism during the Middle Ages, resulted in the emergence of modern science.³ But this commonly held view—that Western thought is a synthesis of *rational* Greek and *irrational* Hebrew—can in no way account for the obsessive recurrence of the will to architecture in philosophy.

For Nietzsche, the Greek side of the equation could not be so easily identified as rational. He writes in *Twilight of the Idols*:

If one needs to make a tyrant of *reason*, as Socrates did, then there must exist no little danger of something else playing the tyrant. Rationality was at that time divined as a *saviour*; neither Socrates nor his "invalids" were free to be rational or not, as they wished—it was *de rigueur*, it was their *last* expedient. The fanaticism with which the whole of Greek thought throws itself at rationality betrays a state of emergency: one was in peril, one had only one choice: either to perish or—be *absurdly rational*. . . . The moralism of the Greek philosophers from Plato downwards is pathologically conditioned: likewise their estimation of dialectics. Reason = virtue = happiness means merely: one must imitate Socrates and counter the dark desires by producing a permanent *daylight*—the daylight of reason. One must be prudent, clear, bright at any cost: every yielding to the instincts, to the unconscious, leads *downwards*.⁴

Nietzsche discovered that the will to architecture, which appears to characterize the West, is itself irrational, despite the appearance that it derives from an ostensibly rational will. Nietzsche's assessment of Christianity as a vulgar Platonism is indeed much more suggestive than the more general view that divides the Hellenic and the Hebraic into a clear-cut dichotomy. One wonders if another origin is veiled behind the origins of the Western as such.

I propose the following view: Plato was no doubt in the minority of Greek thinkers. His belief that architecture could stave off becoming must have appeared abruptly and completely out of the context of Greek thought in general—it must have come from Greece's exterior, from Egypt, where immortality of spirit, monotheism, and state-controlled planning originated. The Platonic notion of the philosopher/king itself can be traced to Egypt.[5] Signs of Egyptian influence can also be discovered at the origins of Judeo-Christianity. Freud, for example, in *Moses and Monotheism*, argued that Moses, who was raised Egyptian and monotheistic, was murdered en route from Egypt.[6] Moses's murder initiated a kind of structure of repetition that Freud called the "return of the repressed." From a Freudian perspective, these two fundamental tenets of Western thought—Judaism and Christianity—originated in Egypt, and it is their origin that has been so strictly repressed and that continues to obsessively return.

My concern here, however, is not with these historical retrospections—not least because they are not persuasive enough to be truly fertile—but with pursuing a totally different line of inquiry, one that is compelled by reconsidering the importance of formalism for the major thinkers of this century. Nietzsche attempted to restore the pre-Socratics—the "philosophers in the tragic age" whom Plato had suppressed.[7] Nietzsche established the prototypical critique of Platonism, but Nietzsche's critique overlooked something: the paradoxical fact— revealed unintentionally by Nietzsche's Platonist contemporaries—that the "will to construct a solid edifice" ultimately does not achieve a foundation, but reveals instead the very absence of its own foundation.

What is overlooked in the return to Nietzsche initiated by poststructuralism is Nietzsche's internalized romanticist disposition; it is from this reconsideration that we are today reinterpreting him. In opposition to reason, romanticists regard as essential the manifold and contingency—immanent in concepts like body, affect, feeling, and the like. But—and this is a point that will be reiterated throughout this study—it is only reason itself that can deconstruct reason. It is my contention that without a formal procedure or method, all critique directed at the will to architecture, no matter how obsessively repeated, will invariably devolve into romanticism.

Plato consistently embraced mathematics as a norm, though not because it provided an architectonic; the mathematics that had been developed in Babylonia and other places was not, for Plato, rigorous, because it was practical and empirical. Plato introduced the proof as *reductio ad absurdum*: if a proposition is agreed upon and established, anything contradictory to it must be avoided as unsound. Euclid developed this framework into an axiomatic system and determined as true only that which is deducible from it. None of these efforts was a sine qua non for mathematical development; on the contrary, they inhibited the algebraic developments that had begun in Babylonia. Mathematics developed, and continues to develop, indifferent to the Platonic desire for architectonicity. What is important to point out here is that Plato fabricated an edifice using as his materials mathematical practices that were not in the least architectonic.

Thus it is in mathematics that the Platonic will to architecture is most often encountered, and, accordingly, it is through mathematics that the critique of Plato must be focused. It is admittedly facile to criticize the *idea* of a horse; to criticize the *idea* of a point is a more serious endeavor because in mathematics something genuinely *ideal* is inevitably exposed. For Nietzsche, mathematics was concerned only with number and quantity, while concept was nothing but a worn-out metaphor.[8] Yet as Marx and others speculated, concept is relation. As a mode of inquiry that scrutinizes the relations of matter, mathematics studies relations that are immutable, relations that never change, regardless of how matter itself changes. Mathematics thus continues to be regarded as the norm it was for Plato.

Here a question emerges: Does the relation of matter exist in the same way that matter exists? Plato was not only the first to pose this question but the first to answer it: he speculated that relation is idea, and therefore relation exists only in the realm of ideas. Though it might appear questionable, this speculation cannot be easily dismissed. If the law of nature is understood as an example of the relation of matter, we might ask, does it follow that this relation exists apart from nature? If it exists at all, where? Modern philosophy sought to locate relation in transcendental subjectivity, and, like Kant, in the a priori form that precedes experience. It was inevitable, then, that those modern philosophers who endeavored to give relation a foundation turned to idealist models, especially given that, as Marx showed, materialism had failed to provide a foundation. In order to deny the significance attributed to the Platonic idea, the ontological status of relation must be reconsidered.

Twentieth-century formalism, which emerged in the midst of these questions, neglected to question the ontological status of relation as such. In mathematics this is prefigured in David Hilbert's formalism. Formalism is marked by its insulation from what one might call the problematic of "to be." Moreover, formalism gives precedence to the arbitrary form that exists irrespective of object or sense, and conversely sees object and sense as interpretation. To be sure, formalism is not restricted to mathematics—it appeared in various fields, and could be described as the fundamental innovation in twentieth-century thought.

Formalism emerged in diverse discursive realms. In linguistics, Ferdinand de Saussure defined language as a form, as a differential system of relation—the signifier is a form, and can thus be anything, including speech, letters, or sign language. What makes language a language is the form, to which sense and objects are only concomitants. This is, of course, parallel to mathematical formalism—structuralist mathematics—from which structuralism emerged.

Given that structure is a transformational rule or function, and not the material form of the object, it is understandable that structuralists emphasized "the invisible structure," where even nothingness functions as a void. This is also reminiscent of Euclidean geometry, where the point, for example, is defined as devoid of spatial expansion: it can be achieved neither in perception nor in imagery but exists only as a relation or a function, as an invisible structure. If so, then where does a structuralist locate the signifier or structure?

When the senses or meanings of words are expelled and signification is understood to exist only in the differential relation, the question emerges, does this relation exist at all? If so, where? Even when structuralists acknowledge only chains of signifier (form), rejecting the Platonic idea as a transcendental signified, the signifier does not exist in the same way as perceptible signs and voices do. Where does it exist? Jacques Lacan locates the Unconscious in a topological space: but where does it exist? Formalists do not question their own "ground." If it is the responsibility of philosophy to question such a ground, it has not shouldered it. Thus, though formalists tacitly return to the Platonic problematic, they carelessly exclude Plato.

Although formalism appeared to have abandoned the Platonic idea, a number of productive working mathematicians—defined precisely by their insistence that relation is a substantial object of mathematical pursuit that need only be discovered—are Platonists even today. Kurt Gödel, who proved the impossibility of formalization precisely by a process of exhaustive formalization, adhered to this view.

Furthermore, formalism takes Plato's "proof" for granted. What is unique about Plato is not, as Nietzsche claimed, that he asserted the existence of an essential world that exists behind the phenomenal world—this view came from Egypt; rather it is that Plato sought the basis for certainty in dialogue, an endeavor that would have been possible only in Athens. As mentioned earlier, axioms are neither a collection of self-evident truths nor matters of empirical fact, but a set of rules necessary in order for there to be dialogue. Rather than taking clear and lucid premises as its point of departure, contemporary axiomatism or formalism enters into a dialogue of mutually agreed upon rules that determine future actions. It could be said, then, that today's axiomatism is based on Plato rather than on Descartes. Moreover, it should be remembered that Plato described Socrates as a figure who ardently abided by the law or the initial agreement, even to the extent that he sacrificed his own life.

It is perhaps symbolic that Plato initiated his *Dialogues* with the murder of Socrates. In subsequent works Socrates assumes various guises, yet even as he does so, we are reminded that he has already been killed. Plato obsessively recounts that Socrates dared to commit suicide to prove the immortality of law. All of this functions, on the one hand, as a presentation of the impossibility of realizing the ideal, and, on the other hand, as a repetitive invocation of this ideal manifest as the will to architecture—a structure that insists on the realization of the impossible. Thus to assert the impossibility of the ideal in no way serves as a real critique of Plato!

The formalist impulse of much twentieth-century thought, based as it was on the precedence of form, was dangerous for those modern philosophers who attempted to ground their studies in transcendental subjectivity. Chief among these was Edmund Husserl. Since he had originally been a mathematician, Husserl was able to grasp precisely the importance of the formalization of mathematics—the theory of sets—that came into existence in the late nineteenth century. Though aware that Husserl's pursuit had opened with *Philosophy of Arithmetic* and closed with *Origin of Geometry*, many phenomenologists ignored the fact that his work had from very early on been focused on mathematics.[1] Indeed, phenomenology, especially in the case of works such as Maurice Merleau-Ponty's *The Phenomenology of Perception* and Ludwig Binswanger's *Phenomenological Psychopathology*, was often regarded as the methodology proper to the "cultural sciences." These phenomenological methodologies follow in the tradition of the neo-Kantian classifications of the "natural and cultural sciences" or Wilhelm Dilthey's hermeneutical classifications, wherein cultural science is dependent upon the understanding (*Verstehen*) and experience (*Erfahrung*) of the subject.

Husserl presented his case as follows: "But now we must note something of the highest importance that

occurred even as early as Galileo: the surreptitious sub-
stitution of the mathematically constructed world of
idealities for the only real world, the one that is actually
given through perception, that is ever experienced and
experienceable—our everyday life-world."[2] Husserl is
not suggesting that we return to the realm of perception
or the life-world; on the contrary, he is seeking to
establish a ground for reason in the age of fascism, over-
powered as it was by romanticist affect and sentiment.
Husserl had descended into the same thought abyss as
Nietzsche had. Both realized that rationality itself is
nothing more than an irrational choice. From the
beginning the "crisis" for Husserl was constantly intertwined with the "crisis of mathematics."

Even the elaboration of syllogistic theory, long enthroned in
the very home territories of philosophy and thought to be
completed long ago, has recently been taken over by mathematicians, in whose hands it has received undreamt of developments. Theories of new types of inference, ignored or
misunderstood by the traditional logic, have at the same time
been discovered and worked out with true mathematical ele-
gance. No one can debar mathematicians from staking claims
to all that can be treated in terms of mathematical form and
method. Only if one is ignorant of the modern science of
mathematics, particularly of formal mathematics, and measures
it by the standards of Euclid or Adam Riese, can one remain
stuck in the common prejudice that the essence of mathematics
lies in number and quantity. It is not the mathematician, but
the philosopher, who oversteps his legitimate sphere when he
attacks "mathematicizing" theories of logic, and refuses to
hand over his temporary foster-children to their natural parents. . . . The scorn with which philosophical logicians like to
speak of mathematical theories of inference, does not alter the
fact that the mathematical form of treatment is in their case (as

in the case of all strictly developed theories in the proper sense of this word) the only scientific one, the only one that offers us systematic closure and completeness, and a survey of all possible questions together with the possible forms of their answers. . . . If the development of all true theories falls in the mathematician's field, what is left over for philosophers?[3]

Husserl knew that the realm that philosophy persisted in regarding as its own was illusory. He was also aware that cultural science and spiritual science were themselves predicated on "the common prejudice that the essence of mathematics lies in number and quantity": in reaction to previous scientific practices, which employed analytical geometry as a model, both cultural science and spiritual science envisioned a way to perceive what other sciences had failed to grasp. Husserl's "crisis" derived from the model or premise on which he based his thinking: formal mathematics would invalidate such divisions as natural and cultural science and general studies and philosophy. Husserl anticipated that formal mathematics would even finally undermine the realm of philosophy proper. Thus from the very first, Husserl's phenomenological research was always accompanied by the question, "What is left over for philosophy (or the philosopher)?"[4]

For Husserl, "what is left over for philosophy" was nothing more than the opportunity to shed light on the ground of the *eidos* or, to borrow Heidegger's term, its "ontological characteristics." Husserl extracts this *eidos* through a phenomenological or *eidetic* reduction. Since the form in formal mathematics exists neither objectively nor psychologically, Husserl holds an epistemological position that is similar to Plato. Husserl claims: "then without doubt we may not reject the self-justifying claims of ideal being. No interpretive skill in the world can in fact eliminate ideal objects from our speech and our thought."[5] Husserl rejects Plato's metaphysical hypostatization—"the assumption that the Species [the *ideal*] really exists *externally* to thought"[6]—just as he rejects the psychological hypostatization—"the assumption that the Species [the *ideal*] really exists *in* thought."[7]

Husserl foresaw that twentieth-century formalism would make inroads not only into mathematics but into every other field of study; today mathematics is found in computer science and molecular biology, among other fields of inquiry. This formalist expansion extended even into the last strongholds of the nineteenth century—into spirit, life, and poetry. Yet the 1930s saw a reaction against formalist expansion: fascism, the political eruption of irrationalism. It was within these ominous conditions that Husserl began to question the status of form. He was situated between the Stalinists, who hoped to rationally construct society itself through the party, and the fascists, who, against the Stalinists, were disposed to unleash their irrational passion. Husserl chose neither.

In Western thought, what is crucial is not the edifice of knowledge itself, but the will to architecture that is renewed with every crisis—a will that is nothing but an irrational choice to establish order and structure within a chaotic and manifold becoming, a will that is only one choice among many. The Husserlian "crisis" not only revives Plato but also reiterates the fact that Western rationalism is a projection (*Entwurf*). But Martin Heidegger radically opposed this resurrection and, for so doing, is subject to the critique that he participated in Nazism.

Today formalism is ubiquitous. No longer useful, perception, affect, nature, life, and the life-world have been dismissed as part of the romanticist reaction against the architectonic. When, in his last years, Heidegger asked, "What does it mean that philosophy in the present age has entered its final stage?,"[8] he was attempting to think the problem of cybernetics.

No prophecy is necessary to recognize that the sciences now establishing themselves will soon be determined and steered by the new fundamental science which is called cybernetics.

This science corresponds to the determination of man as an acting social being. For it is the theory of the steering of the possible planning and arrangement of human labor. Cybernetics transforms language into an exchange of news. The arts become regulated-regulating instruments of information.

The development of philosophy into the independent sciences which, however, interdependently communicate among themselves ever more markedly, is the legitimate completion of philosophy. Philosophy is ending in the present age.[9]

Judging from this citation, it is not clear that Heidegger was fully aware of the important role that cybernetics would play in twentieth-century intellectual developments; rather, he appears to have considered it nothing more than a new technology. Cybernetics functions as a nullifier of traditional dichotomies such as material/life and animal/human by reconstructing everything as difference/information; it is the horizon where "spirit" and "human" can no longer play their privileged, a priori roles. As Heidegger asserted, philosophy grounded in such values "is ending in the present age."

With this in mind, Heidegger's question—"What task is reserved for thinking at the end of philosophy?"[10] —begins to make sense. Indeed, it can be understood as a question that succeeds Husserl's. Heidegger insists that the cybernetic is ontic, and therefore what is reserved for philosophy is no longer ontological problems. What is left for philosophy is precisely *not* what consciousness and reason have excluded. (One need only recall that Jacques Lacan formalized the "unconscious" mathematically.) Thus, a philosophy that gives priority to relation over substance and difference over identity is already a science, or rather, already a common state of affairs. Our concern is not with the speculative, but with the actualized "philosophy of difference"; we are no longer allowed to speak positively about the sense in which mankind sustains its *humanness* in contrast to the realized formal system—the computer. Instead we understand that that which makes mankind human (the ground for humanness) lies in its ungroundedness (*Abgründlichkeit*).[11]

If we approach Heidegger's question sympathetically, it can be read, like Husserl's, as one concerned with a new formalism. In this context, it is understandable that despite his keen admiration for Nietzsche, Heidegger criticized Nietzsche for remaining within the philosophy of subjectivity and, paradoxically, praised Plato as a philosopher who had grasped "Being" as idea. Actualized formalism forbids the presupposition of subjectivity, body, or the like. Furthermore, any critique of formalism, if executed indifferent to this actual condition, is destined to return to some kind of preformalist position. It could be argued that something like this occurs in Jacques Derrida's development of deconstruction. Derrida's critique of Husserl, particularly his development of grammatology, was not dependent on literary categories. Rather, Derrida was more concerned with categories developed in fields such as contemporary molecular biology, in which genes are arranged in alternate pairings of a quartet of chromosomatic *écritures*.

Unlike Heidegger, Derrida would never ask, "What is reserved for philosophy?" Instead, he asks, "What has allowed philosophy to endure for so long?" But this too is a philosophical question. Amidst all of the formalization that comprises the formalization of philosophy itself, we must question not only whether the form exists but also where it exists and whether and where the exteriority of the form exists. To do so we must again confront Plato's choice.

Plato banished poets from his state because they did not understand the products of their own making and as a result would damage language itself. Late eighteenth-century romanticism forever altered the relationship between philosophy and poetry. Romanticism gave a legitimacy to the cognitive drives of the body, to sense, emotion, passion, and so forth, all of which were favored over formal knowledge. Hegel integrated this contradictory relationship between reason and sensuality into his account of *Geist*, or world spirit, and in the process he *aestheticized* reason itself. Aesthetics, the name given to this privileging of the cognitive impulses of the body, was understood to mediate between reason and sensuality.

Does this mean that after the long exile imposed by Plato poets finally seized control? On the contrary, the opposite occurred: poetry itself was absorbed into, and became a division of, philosophy. The romanticist illusion—which holds that poetry is more primordial than philosophy, and therefore amounts to a criticism of Platonic philosophy—persists even today. Yet it was precisely those poets who insisted on making (*poiesis*) who criticized aesthetics. It was those poets who, in other words, took up the Platonic position that had originally ousted them—a group of poets from Edgar Allan Poe to Paul Valéry—who attempted to make poetry architectonic by rejecting becoming.

In rejecting romanticist inspiration, Poe sought to construct poetry rationally. In his essay "Notes Nouvelles sur Poe," Charles Baudelaire stressed his own constructive precisionism by citing Poe's statement that he faced his making with the rigorous precision and logic of mathematics. It was Valéry, however, who realized that the awareness of the mystical process of poetry—*poiesis* in the narrow sense—leads to the speculation of *techné* in a broad sense. In his *Eupalinos, or the Architect*, Valéry very clearly defines the poet as an architect. Poets once exiled by Plato could now return armed with the Platonic will to architecture, if only to expose the limits of architecture itself.[1] Valéry writes elsewhere:

I look *for the first time* at this thing I have found. I note what I have said about its form, and I am perplexed. Then I ask myself the question: *Who made this?*

Who made this? asks the naive moment.

My first stir of thought has been to think of *making*.

The idea of *making* is the first and most human of ideas.

"To explain" is never anything more than to describe a way of *making*: it is merely to remake in thought. The *why* and the *how*, which are only ways of expressing the implications of this idea, inject themselves into every statement, demanding satisfaction at all costs. Metaphysics and science are merely an *unlimited* development of this demand.[2]

But this question—"Who made this?"—should not be "answered." It is a question that is demanded by the position of making itself, a question that in reality suggests the absence of the author. "Whenever we run across something we do not know how to make but that appears to be made, we say that nature produced it."[3] Here, Valéry is not comparing man and nature, but is instead provisionally proposing the name "nature" to identify the limitations or impossibilities that are encountered in the course of the exhaustive pursuit of making.

Nature, therefore, is not restricted to ostensibly natural objects such as the seashell; it also includes things that are made by man but whose structure—how they are made—is not immediately discernible. Such things are called natural language because their making is not apparent. It is in this exact sense that Marx, in his introduction to *Capital*, insisted upon seeing history as natural history. Marx's "natural history" is unlike the Hegelian *Geist* that subsumes all making. (It is important to note that neither does natural history attempt to explain everything through dialectical materialism.) "Natural" indicates everything that we do not know how to make. It is only by determining what man makes that we can begin to shed light on what nature makes. Valéry writes:

> In general, if we examine a man-made object, if we consider its form, its *external structure*, and compare it to the *internal structure*, we should find a relation which is not the same as the relation we find between the internal and external structures of a so-called *natural* object, whether geological or organic. I do not claim that the problem can always be solved; there are ambiguous cases, but quite frequently we find—on superficial examination, without the aid of a microscope—that in the human work the structure of the internal parts seems less important than the *form* of the assemblage. Thus the human work, regardless of its material, would seem to be an assemblage whose manipulator takes very little account of the internal structure of the thing he is fashioning. You can make similar things with very different materials; regardless of whether a vase be of glass, metal, or porcelain, it can assume pretty much the same form, but this

means that (except during the actual process of manufacture) you have disregarded the *material* of which you have made the vase. Moreover, if you continue to examine the man-made object, you find that the form of the whole is *less complex* than the internal structure of the parts, and this suggests a disarrangement. In this sense, *order* imposes *disorder*. I recall that I once took this example: if you line up a regiment, you obtain a geometric figure composed of elements, each of which is far more complex than the whole, since each one is a man. Similarly, if you make an article of furniture, you disturb the organization of the tree, for you cut it up and reassemble the pieces without concern for its internal structure. The wood provides you with stable elements which you can consider as invariable in relation to the forms and contours you give the assemblage.[4]

Valéry notes that the mark of what man makes is found in the simplicity of the structure of its form as compared to the structure or composition of its material. When the structure of a literary work is grasped, for instance, it is always simpler than the text itself; although it is made by man, the text is more complex and excessive than the structure because it is a composite construction of the natural material of language. On the other hand, no structure can exist apart from a certain purposefulness in its own formation. A hidden meaning, or an author, is always presupposed in any structural analysis of a text.

Instead of describing "what nature makes," Valéry exposes it as something that is irreducible to the structures that we construct in our thinking: Valéry understands making as something that is always in excess of structure. It is important that Valéry, a poet, did not resort to the primordial position of poetic imagination, and that he attempted instead to approach the impossibility of architecture from the position of construction. In this chapter, I wish to offer the example of an architect/planner, Christopher Alexander, who continued—perhaps unintentionally—to pursue the Valerian question.

Alexander calls those cities that have emerged over the course of many years natural cities. He does this in order to distinguish them from artificial cities, which have been deliberately created by designers and planners. He argues that artificial cities lack the essential ingredients of cities. It is thus not unreasonable, he asserts, that people are becoming more and more reluctant to accept these thoroughly planned metropolises. As he points out, many designers have attempted to enliven modern-style artificial cities by introducing the ingredients of natural cities; those attempts have so far been unsuccessful because they have failed to grasp the inner structure of the city itself and have instead imitated the appearance or image of the natural city. Alexander maintains

a

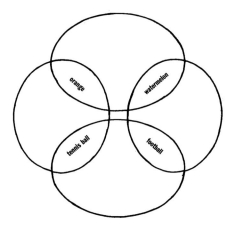

b

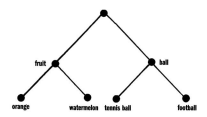

c

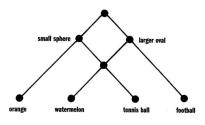

d

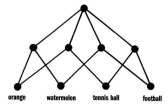

that the natural city is organized in the form of a semi-lattice, whereas the artificial city is organized in the form of a tree.

Both tree and semi-lattice offer ways of conceptualizing how various small systems interact to form large complex systems. Generally speaking, tree and semi-lattice describe different denominations for the structures of order within a set. For example, suppose that we must sort into two groups an orange, a watermelon, a football, and a tennis ball. One way is to sort the two fruits together, the orange and the watermelon, and the two balls together, the football and the tennis ball. Another is to sort them according to shape: the two small spheres, the orange and the tennis ball, and the two larger oblong objects, the watermelon and the football. Taken individually, either sorting forms a tree structure (figure 1b, c). But when the two sortings are combined, they result in a semi-lattice (figure 1d); if presented in the language of set theory, the figure would appear as 1a. In these latter examples of the semi-lattice, however, it is harder to visualize all four sets simultaneously. It is similarly difficult to visualize the semi-lattice structure—where multiple sets overlap—of the natural city, and thus we tend to reduce it to a tree, the only structure we can visualize.

Alexander describes the semi-lattice structure of a natural city as follows: "In Berkeley, at the corner of Hearst and Euclid, there is a drug store, and outside the drug store a traffic light. In the entrance to the drug store there is a news rack where the day's papers are displayed."[1] These are unchanging elements in the city; and yet, while standing and waiting during a red light, people look at the papers or buy them. When these three elements are combined they begin to function differently. Through human use these ensembles form a unit of

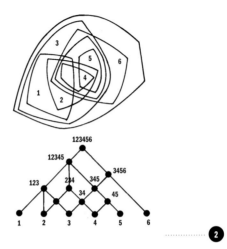

the city. Continuing, Alexander writes:

[The city] derives its coherence as a unit both from the forces which hold its own elements together, and from the dynamic coherence of the larger *living system* which includes it as a fixed, invariant part. . . . Of the many, many fixed concrete subsets of the city which are the receptacles for its systems, and can therefore be thought of as significant physical units, we usually single out a few for special consideration. . . . A collection of subsets which goes to make up such a picture is not merely an amorphous collection. Automatically, merely because relationships are established among the subsets once the subsets are chosen, the collection has a definite structure. . . . Instead of talking about the real sets of millions of real particles which occur in the city, let us consider a simpler structure made of just half a dozen elements.[2]

The visualization of such, figure 2, is in this case a semi-lattice. "A collection of sets forms a semi-lattice if and only if, when two overlapping sets belong to the collec-

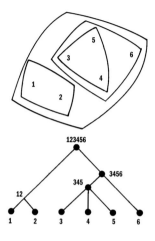

123456

3456

345

12

1   2   3   4   5   6

3

tion, then the set of elements common to both also belongs to the collection."[3] In figure 2, for example, both sets (2,3,4) and (3,4,5) belong to the collection, as does their common area (3,4). As far as the city is concerned, when the two units overlap, the overlapping area is itself a recognizable entity and hence a unit as well. As applied to the previous example, one unit would consist of the news rack, sidewalk, and traffic light, and the other of the drug store itself, with its entry and the news rack. The two units then overlap in the domain of the news rack and this overlapping area would itself be a recognizable unit. The structure of this collection is therefore defined as a semi-lattice. In artificial cities these overlappings are nonexistent.

As opposed to the semi-lattice, a tree is defined as follows: "A collection of sets forms a tree if and only if, for any two sets that belong to the collection, either one is wholly contained in the other, or else they are wholly disjoint."[4] Figure 3 illustrates the tree structure where no overlapping occurs.

Alexander further elaborates the distinction between the two by pointing out that the semi-lattice has a greater potential of developing into a more complex and subtle structure. A tree based on 20 elements can contain only 19 subsets, while a semi-lattice based on 20 elements can contain more than a million different subsets. Yet we tend to reduce natural structures, structures that are without exception semi-lattices, to tree structures, because a tree offers us a simple and distinct mechanism to divide a complex entity into units. It is because of their tree structure that artificial cities lack structural complexity. Alexander analyzes nine well-known city plans—both executed and proposed—for Brasília and Tokyo, among others, and finds that all are based on the tree structure; without exception, the tree principle is so dominant that no single element can connect itself with any other independent of the mediation of the unit as a whole.

Alexander's mathematical examination of the difference between artificial cities and natural cities is so suggestive precisely because it is formal. Moreover, it can be expanded to include institutional organizations. In military or bureaucratic organizations, for example, where the network is structured like a tree, transverse intercourse—except through headquarters—is never allowed (figure 4, top). When we observe how organizations actually function, we see that the tree structure is often modified. Since communication must occur more or less transversally, bureaucratic organizations often adopt the semi-lattice in their actual functioning. It is in spy and underground organizations that the most typical tree structure must be rigidly maintained; each member is allowed to communicate only with a higher level of management, so that no transverse connection between members is possible. On the other hand, rela-

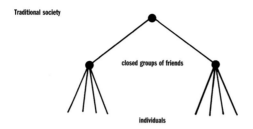

Traditional society

closed groups of friends

individuals

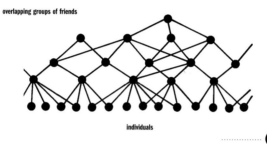

Open society

overlapping groups of friends

individuals

4

tionships between friends and acquaintances in an open society form the semi-lattice, as shown in figure 4, bottom.

According to Alexander, both city and social organization would be devastated if the tree structure were followed too strictly; contemporary city planning has essentially followed this course, and the consequences are well documented in cities like Brasília. Alexander writes, "In any organized object, extreme compartmentalization and the dissociation of internal elements are the first signs of coming destruction. In a society, dissociation is anarchy. In a person, dissociation is the mark of schizophrenia and impending suicide."[5]

Alexander's view of the city is strikingly different from the views of those who, in the name of sustaining a livable, humane urban space, object to city planning. This is because for Alexander the natural city is a "city which nature made." Alexander does not glorify nature, nor does he oppose it to the man-made. His critique of the architectural attempts of city planners notwithstanding, Alexander is the thinker who takes city planning into account in the most architectonic manner.

Inasmuch as the early twentieth-century modernists are the embodiment of the Platonic philosopher/king, Alexander's criticism amounts to a fundamental proof of the impossibility of the Platonic ideal. His methodology, however, continues to be informed by the Platonic will to architecture; rather than resorting to the illusion of nature as exterior to the man-made, it reveals the exterior as a negative figure at the heart of the man-made.

Five **Structure and Zero**

Alexander's work has developed in parallel with approaches in other disciplines. One could cite the mathematical structuralism of Bourbaki—the pseudonym of a group of French structuralist mathematicians. Bourbaki's operational method consisted of an initial reduction of all data to sets, and then the reestablishment of these set elements as structure. This structure is composed of three categories: algebraic structures, structures of order, and topological structures. Whereas the structuralism known through the works of Roman Jakobson and Claude Lévi-Strauss relies mainly on algebraic structure, Alexander employs the "structures of order" of sets.

Structuralism became known to the general public through linguistics, especially the phonology of Jakobson, which drastically diverged from the linguistics of Ferdinand de Saussure. Saussure maintained that "in language there are only differences, and *without positive terms*."[1] Jakobson proposed an alternative approach that argued for the systematization of the very phonetic organization that Saussure had left jumbled. This would be accomplished by rethinking the organizational structure as sets of binary oppositions.

It is not only the differences between the vocalic phonemes of Turkish which are resolvable into simple and indivisible binary oppositions, but all the differences between all the phonemes of every language. It follows that all the phonemes of each particular language, both the vowels and the consonants, can be dissociated into non-decomposable *distinctive features*. The apparent contradictions are now removed. The oppositions of such differential qualities are real binary oppositions, as defined in logic, i.e., they are such that each of the terms of the opposition *necessarily* implies its opposite. Thus, the idea of closure is opposed only by the idea of openness; the front and back features mutually imply each other, and so on.[2]

The phonetic organization, which once seemed so confused, could henceforth be grasped as quite orderly, though still complex. Lévi-Strauss was inspired by this assertion of the orderly composition of chaos. "Structural linguistics will certainly play the same renovating role with respect to the social sciences that nuclear physics, for example, has played for the physical sciences."[3] The remarkable success of phonology, however, owes largely to its application of mathematical structure. It was his development of mathematical structure, in fact, that made it possible for Jakobson to formally compose that which had seemed too jumbled or chaotic for our intellect to reconstruct—he enabled us to see, explicitly, the structure of "what nature makes."

Lévi-Strauss made use of Kleinian algebraic structures in his analysis of the kinship structures among uncivilized societies. And yet, to return to Valéry, "what nature makes" is much more complex than what man reconstructs, because the structure of what man reconstructs is formed only by way of certain predetermined objectives. Underscoring this, Jakobson writes:

Modern specialists in the field of acoustics wonder with bewilderment how it is possible that the human ear has no difficulty in recognizing the great variety of sounds in a language given that they are so numerous and their variations so imperceptible. Can it really be that it is a purely auditory faculty that is involved here? No, not at all! What we recognize in spoken language is not sound differences in themselves but the different uses to which they are put by the language, i.e., differences which, though without meaning in themselves, are used in discriminating one from another entities of a higher level (morphemes, words).[4]

Sound pattern is not equal to speech sound: it is a form that can exist differentially only if a higher classificatory meta-level is presumed. The same can be said with regard to morpheme, word, and clause; each is equally extractable as a differential form only when a higher level is presupposed for each classification. Saussure stressed that *langue* is a social fact that exists independent of the speaking subject. However, herein lies a paradox: sound pattern—as distinguished from physical speech sound—can be extracted only so long as there is a distinctive function, but above all it exists only if there is a speaking subject. In other words, whenever meaning for the subject of speech exists, the form that distinguishes it is understood to be preexistent, and not vice versa. In this way, the linguistics of *langue* is constituted by the phenomenological reduction that begins with the consciousness of the subject of speech. It is extracted by the reduction or bracketing, for instance, of physical speech sound, referents, and contexts. Thus the linguistics of *langue* requires, as its premise, the subject. It is for that reason that the differential form thereby discovered is invariably teleological in that it presupposes a higher level of organization. As Valéry pointed out with respect to "what man makes," it is always accompanied by simplification.

We can discern an isomorphic relationship in Alexander. Let us look again at the example of the news rack at the intersection. This news rack already functions as an overlap and can therefore function as a recognizable unit. However, if transferred to another location, it might not function in the same way. The structure of the natural city thus emerges from the consciousness of the "subject living in the city," and the semiotics of the city or of architecture comes into being when objects like the traffic light and news rack are seen merely as differential forms; specifically, they are forms extracted by a phenomenological reduction of the "world-being-lived."

Structure, therefore, presupposes the transcendental ego with which it integrates itself. Herein lies the reason Derrida initiated his critique—deconstruction—

with his reading of Husserlian phenomenology and not of structuralism. Structuralists abandoned the ego because they had discovered an apparatus by means of which to lump the excess beyond "what man makes" into structure: zero. Jakobson introduced this zero in order to complete his phonemic system.

A zero-phoneme . . . is opposed to all other French phonemes by the absence both of distinctive features and of a constant sound characteristic. On the other hand, the zero-phoneme ∂ is opposed to the absence of any phoneme whatsoever.[5]

In the field of mathematics the zero sign is a common-place. Mathematical structure is at work as a function rather than a form; in its rules of transformation, even a function that is not transformational must be included. Jakobson's zero phoneme corresponds to the unit element e in mathematical transformation groups. Thus it is only natural that Jakobson would employ zero, for he focused on the bundles of oppositional relationships *between* phonemes rather than on the individual phonemes themselves as structure; only with the introduction of zero can a group (structure) be constituted. For Jakobson, zero meant no more and no less.

Zero was invented in India and was originally the name for *not* moving a bead on an abacus. If it were not for zero, the numbers 205 and 25 would be indistinguishable. In other words, zero is "opposed to the absence of any *number* whatsoever." The place-value system was thus established by the introduction of zero. Even though in Sanskrit the word for zero is the same as the word for the Buddhist concept of emptiness, "zero" must be distinguished from this metaphysical concept, for it was introduced for practical and technical purposes. However, considering that zero was accepted much more readily in India than in the West—where its debut in the twelfth century caused great panic—these concepts might well have been connected. In his essay on Edgar Allan Poe, Mallarmé wrote this about the role of zero:

> The intellectual armature of a poem hides and remains—takes place—in the space that isolates the stanzas and amid the margins of the paper: such a significant silence that it is no less crucial to compose than the verses themselves.[6]

It has been recognized that Mallarmé's "margin" was derived from Lao Tzu's phrase "nothing as useful."[7] Rather than functioning as pure zero, both concepts are philosophical, whereas Jakobson's zero sign is a technical device, a sheer theoretical sine qua non that enables one to constitute a structure. In any event, once introduced technically, zero inevitably induces further reflection. Gilles Deleuze has observed that "structuralism is inseparable from a new kind of transcendental philosophy, where places surpass what occupies them."[8] It is indeed possible that such a philosophy had already been introduced in the place-value system, in which case structuralism emerged precisely with the introduction of the zero sign.

Zero did not remain a purely technical instrument. With Lévi-Strauss's Jakobson-inspired (zero phoneme) structuralist interpretation of Marcel Mauss's notions of *mana* (in *Esquise d'une théorie générale de la magie*) and *hau* (in *Essai sur le don*), which had introduced the zero sign in anthropology, zero became saturated with philosophical connotations. In the native Polynesian *hau*, Mauss thought he had discovered a faculty that compelled a reciprocity of gift/exchange. Lévi-Strauss, however, could not accept Mauss's methodological approach, which was reliant on the natives' consciousness, and suggested instead the transcendental categories *hau* or *mana*. Learning from Jakobson's zero phoneme, Lévi-Strauss redefined the notion of the *mana* type as "in itself devoid of meaning and thus susceptible of receiving any meaning at all."[9] Lévi-Strauss identified this zero sign as a floating signifier.

This is exactly like the empty space in a puzzle of shifting numbers or letters that allows the pieces to be shifted around into some kind of order. What drives the movement of the game is not the differential system of signifiers, the 1, 2, 3, but the empty lot itself. While a player may think that she or he is relocating numbers, from another point of view it is the empty lot that is floating around and that enables this movement. To put it in the language of Lacan: while each number thinks that it is the subject, it is nothing but an effect of this floating signifier. No matter how radical this reversal may be, it must be noted that the floating signifier, or zero sign, guarantees the structurality of structure and, thus, exists merely as a proxy for God or the transcendental ego.

To take *mana* as the zero sign is equal to taking the zero sign as *mana*. In the Jodo sect of Buddhism, the transcendental other—the object of worship—is regarded merely as a representation of absolute emptiness.[10] In this regard, the Jodo sect, which asks the transcendental other for salvation, and the Zen school, which aims at achieving *satya* unaided, are not as distant from each other as they might seem. In China, they coexisted under the roof of the same temple—Zen was the teaching formulated specifically for intellectuals, and the Jodo sect was for the general public. Likewise, in both the

Judaic cabbalah and in Islamic mysticism, the anthropomorphic God is merely a representation contrived for the public. The invocation of zero amounts not to the abrogation of the transcendent, however, but to its replacement. Such a discourse—that it is not the subject but emptiness that makes, or that even the subject itself is made by emptiness—is thus simply a replacement for the proposition that it is God who makes.

The signified of a signifier is another signifier, and thus meaning as such does not exist; instead, there is only a chain of signifiers. Roland Barthes observed that in the West, as one traces the chain of signifiers, one encounters the ultimate signifier—God. God, then, closes the infinitely retrogressive chain and, by so doing, completes the sign system. To put it another way, all sign systems must presuppose this ultimate signifier: zero as the negation of absence. Barthes proposed to introduce the empty sign or sign degree zero in order to emancipate signifiers from the domination of the ultimate signified. He discovered an *Empire of Signs* in Japan, though it should be understood that this ideal model of Japan is nothing but a representation of the Western mind.[11]

Resorting to zero does not do away with the transcendental being, but instead replaces it. Zero is the sine qua non for the maintenance of structure; it is where the phenomenological *cogito* resides. Lacan would no doubt attack this use of zero, but his alternative was merely to replace it with the function of lack or emptiness. It was Derrida who foresaw that to go beyond the phenomenological subject or transcendental ego through the structuralist strategy was illusory; on this basis he initiated his critique of phenomenology. This does not mean that Derrida sides with structuralism by critiquing phenomenology. Instead, he acknowledges the "superiority of phenomenology," only to then deconstruct it. Derrida reveals the concealed operation of *différance*, in which nonpresence enables the privileged "presence" in phenomenology; structure understood as presence is always enclosed, because such a structure suppresses the inevitable movement of *différance*. What then is this inevitable *différance?* As we will see, it is nothing but the self-referentiality of the structure or formal system itself.

Alexander shows that no matter how complex or chaotic structure appears, the only model of that structure we are capable of producing is the tree. Furthermore, he insists that the manifold nature of the semi-lattice is based on a univocalization. Not only the tree structure but even the semi-lattice is incontestably simpler than Valéry's notion of "what nature makes." To put it another way, some things that have the characteristics of "what nature makes" are really made by man, though the process of their making is not clear or obvious. Because of these "natural" characteristics, man cannot be the true subject of their making. Accordingly, the attributes that Alexander identifies with the natural city fall into the category of the idiomatic adjective "natural"—natural language, natural number, and natural (as opposed to artificial) intelligence.

Six **Natural Numbers**

We need not pit nature or literature against structuralism. Even though poststructuralism is often understood as a return to the natural, it is only by giving in to the will to architecture that the potential deconstructive effects of poststructuralism can be fully understood and developed. It is ironic that in the history of Western thought, only the most rigorous attempts to be constructive have produced, rather than a grounded construction, its antithesis. Paul de Man, for example, shows how

John Locke, who sought the most rigorous use of language, was the first to raise the issue of figural or natural language.

And indeed, when Locke then develops his own theory of words and language, what he constructs turns out to be in fact a theory of tropes. Of course, he would be the last man in the world to realize and to acknowledge this. One has to read him, to some extent, against or regardless of his own explicit statements; one especially has to disregard the commonplaces about his philosophy that circulate as reliable currency in the intellectual histories of the Enlightenment. One has to pretend to read him ahistorically, the first and necessary condition if there is to be any expectation of ever arriving at a somewhat reliable history. That is to say, he has to be read not in terms of explicit statements (especially explicit statements about statements) but in terms of the rhetorical motions of his own text, which cannot be simply reduced to intentions or to identifiable facts.[1]

De Man's characteristically deconstructive reading makes clear that only a philosophy that rejects rhetoric can truly understand it. Accordingly, only insofar as he pursues "the rigorous uses of language" do Locke's texts develop an account of figure. Locke's constructive or architectural will in turn reveals its inversion, just as the Euclidean principle that sought architectonic precision disclosed non-Euclidean geometry. The paradox exposed by de Man's reading of Locke is constituted only where the will to architecture is explicitly engaged.

Elsewhere, de Man examines the well-known poem by William Butler Yeats that concludes with the line "How can we know the dancer from the dance?" This line has often been interpreted as the rhetorical question "How we can distinguish the dancer from the dance?," implying the indivisibility of form and experience, creator and creation, sign and referent. If read literally, however, it asks, "[Please tell me] how to distinguish the dancer from the dance," resulting in an inversion of the previous reading. In this sentence, two consistent but incongruous ways of reading coexist, neither of which is superior to the other. M. C. Escher's drawings provide a visual analogy of this situation: as one's focal point shifts, figure and ground fluctuate indefinitely between positive and negative.

In this way, de Man proves the undecidability of textual meaning. However, offering a proof with respect to the essentially ambiguous literary text is easily misunderstood: on the one hand, this sort of proof tends to be assimilated to the idea of poetic ambiguity, due to its conventional distrust of philosophy; on the other, it is also confronted by the general antipathy to formalism. De Man addresses this issue as follows:

On the other hand—and this is the real mystery—no literary formalism, no matter how accurate and enriching in its analytic powers, is ever allowed to come into being without seeming reductive. When form is considered to be the external trappings of literary meaning or content, it seems superficial and expendable. The development of intrinsic, formalist criticism in the twentieth century has changed this model: form is now a solipsistic category of self-reflection, and the referential meaning is said to be extrinsic. The polarities of inside and outside have been reversed, but they are still the same polarities that are at play: internal meaning has become outside reference, and the outer form has become the intrinsic structure. A new version of reductiveness at once follows this reversal: formalism nowadays is mostly described in an imagery of imprisonment and claustrophobia: the "prison house of language," "the impasse of formalist criticism," etc.[2]

Formalism is repudiated because it is still understood as it was in the nineteenth century. Such a limited understanding, though, encourages us to return to the content or the object, to the exterior of form. As we have seen, formalism has affected every discipline. Literature, especially, is a realm where "formalization" has been and can be executed only in an arbitrary fashion, and this outcome provides many with a pretext to criticize formalization itself. Though the methodological simplicity of structuralist literary criticism is all too apparent, one cannot dismiss the importance of structuralism, nor its formalist impulse. Indeed, the ambiguity of the text becomes problematic only insofar as the structuralist will to architecture is understood to be preexistent; moreover, it is revealed only by means of the paradox that the structuralist desire to systematize or rationalize produces the unintended opposite effect. The ambiguity of the text can only be fully understood by formalization, and not by historical retrospection.

First and foremost, a deconstruction of the architectonic must be focused on the very realm in which the architectonic or construction seems to be most unassailably constituted, that is, in mathematics. Moreover, as indicated by two facts—that what Valéry was meditating upon during his long public silence were the problems of contemporary mathematics provoked by Henri Poincaré, and that structuralism originally stemmed from the mathematics of Bourbaki—we must recognize that underlying all of the issues I have been reviewing were the problematics of mathematical formalization that date to the late nineteenth century. It is thus imperative that we begin our speculation with mathematical problems.

Within the field of nineteenth-century geometry it was understood that the Platonic and Euclidean attempt to turn mathematics into an axiomatic architecture was inconsistent with respect to "the fifth postulate" (of parallel lines). While developing the postulate, Euclid had relied on apperceptual self-evidence. But according to Euclid's principle, a postulate must be constituted independent of apperceptual self-evidence; otherwise it cannot serve as the foundation of a solid edifice. Euclid defined a point as devoid of spatial expansion; and it is precisely because it is not a perceptible object with a spatial dimension that it can be a foundation for a mathematical edifice. Conversely, since the parallel postulate does not provide a solid foundation, mathematicians have long questioned its status, repeating the futile attempt to deduce it as a theorem from the other Euclidean postulates.

Since it was discovered that a non-Euclidean geometry could be established by introducing the postulate "parallel lines intersect," faith in mathematical architectonicity has been fundamentally shaken. The flaw in Euclid's work lies in his reliance on perception, or natural language, and in his inference of the straight line and point. On the other hand, non-Euclidean geometry made it clear that mathematics could exist independent from reality or perception; in one sense, this constituted a move toward a more rigorous formalization of mathematics.

Though somewhat connected to the challenge of non-Euclidean geometry, the early twentieth-century crisis in mathematics began with the development of the theory of sets. From the moment Descartes defined points as coordinates of numbers, the point and line segment in geometry became an issue of numbers. For a line segment to be continuous, no matter how short it may be, there must exist an infinite number of infinitely minute points along the line; the numbers corresponding to these points are called real numbers, though in essence they are *imaginary*. George Cantor's theory of sets was formulated in order to deal with this kind of infinity. Cantor saw infinity not as limitless but as a number. With this, the paradox of set theory emerged, which can be described as follows: if we grant the theorem "Given any set, finite or infinite, a set with more elements can always be obtained," then the moment one considers "the set of all the possible elements," a contradiction arises.

Bertrand Russell transformed this paradox into the simpler form of the well-known paradox of Epimenides: "'All Cretans are liars,' said a Cretan." Simplified further it becomes "I am lying" or "This sentence is false." In all cases it is equally indeterminable whether the statement is true or false. In this way, various forms of paradox were discovered and named; yet they invariably occurred in sentences with a self-referential structure. Russell therefore insisted that paradoxes were caused by a state of confusion wherein "class" itself becomes its own "member." Paradoxes could be avoided if this mix-up were prohibited. Russell subsequently established the order of logical types and prohibited confusing them.

Independent of these developments, Frank Plumpton Ramsey identified two distinct kinds of paradox that Russell had previously regarded as one and the same: the paradox of the "set that includes itself" and that of "Epimenides's liar." Ramsey criticized Russell by observing that the former proposition can be solved by logical typing, but not the latter. As long as this latter proposition primarily concerns a way of phrasing, it is irrelevant to logical typing and irresolvable within the logical system. In another development, Alfred Talski classified the levels of language and established what he called higher language by observing the logical system from its exterior. By considering that value judgment—the definition of truth—exists exterior to the logical system, he named the propositional system that becomes the object of value judgment "object-language" and the system that contains value judgment itself "meta-language." Moreover, a "meta-meta-language" is required whenever a meta-criticism of meta-language is required. This elaborate system of typing was originally formulated to avoid paradox, but, as Gödel demonstrated, the primary contradiction recurs with every attempt to prevent contradiction.

As we have already seen, the aporias that result from the theory of sets and from geometry are essentially the same. Real numbers are described, after all, by natural numbers. For example, that a real number, 0.24910370 . . . , is described by the natural numbers 0, 2, 4, 9 . . . proves that natural numbers are fundamental. However, since Cantor, set theory has attempted to formalize natural numbers according to sets. For example, assume zero is an empty set ($\emptyset$); then, when 1 is an empty set, 2 will be an empty set, and so on. It was Gödel's proof that exposed the impossibility of giving a foundation to natural numbers by such a procedure. The problematic of perception and form in geometry was thus replaced by that of natural numbers and their formalization, equating the founding of Euclidean geometry with the founding of natural numbers.

Intuitionists criticized logicists such as Russell, who regarded mathematics as a subgenre of logic, noting that paradox arises as a result of the use of nondescript entities such as real numbers. Intuitionists thus determined to restrict mathematics and to focus only on the ways it is affected and made operable by "intuition." A completely different approach was subsequently introduced by David Hilbert. Hilbert's formalist approach sought to render mathematics genuinely independent of perception. By depleting the axiom of all intuitive meaning, Hilbert formalized mathematics as a nonsensical collection of symbols or formulas and their transformational rules of inference. For Hilbert the meaning of the axiom is not questioned; it no longer requires intuitive self-evidence. Rather, what matters is the qualification of the propositions that form an axiom and, upon acceptance of such propositions, what type of axiomatic system is constituted. In order to establish a consistent mathematical system based purely upon logical concepts, logicists had to take as a premise the not necessarily logical axiom of infinity. For Hilbert, however, to the extent that the axiomatic system is free of inconsistency, any system—including even the axiom of infinity—can be taken as a premise.

In this way, Hilbert discovered the solid foundation of mathematics in the consistency of its formal system: mathematics does not have to be "true" as long as it is "consistent," and as long as this is the case, there is no need for further foundation. As a consequence, proof of consistency in the formalized axiomatic system becomes crucial. One way to insure consistency is to resort to an intuitive model, as in the case of Riemannian geometry: if one regards the plane as a sphere in Euclidean geometry, the point as a point on the sphere, and the straight line as a great circle arc in its system of axioms, the sphere of Euclidean geometry becomes the primordial model. By so doing, every axiom of Riemannian geometry can be translated into a theorem in Euclidean geometry. As long as Euclidean geometry is consistent, non-Euclidean geometry should also be consistent. And yet, because it relies on "intuition," the consistency of Euclidean geometry cannot be proven internally.

The crux of Hilbert's formalist approach lies in his decision to give up such a method altogether. He distinguished the system of axioms from the logic that proves its consistency, and called the latter "meta-mathematics." To avoid mathematical contradiction, and in order to satisfy even the intuitionists, Hilbert designed his approach to be finite and compositional. Yet just as Hilbert's method seemed to be emerging as a success, Gödel's incompleteness theorem arrived to deal it a fatal blow.

The incompleteness theorem can be outlined as follows: insofar as the axiomatic system achieved by formalizing the theory of natural numbers is consistent, it can be understood as neither provable nor disprovable with regard to the system. Hence, an undecidable formula always exists. In addition, the theorem includes the following thesis: "Even if a theory T, that includes the natural number theory, is consistent, its proof cannot be achieved within T; a theory stronger than T is required."

Because Gödel's proof is well known, I will not explain it in much detail here. Put simply, by arithmetizing meta-mathematics (which he accomplished by translating the symbols of meta-mathematics into natural numbers, called Gödel's numbers) Gödel discovered a cyclical and seemingly self-enclosed movement (see figure 5). By means of this calculation he ingeniously set up a self-referential paradox wherein meta-mathematics, understood as a class, gets mixed into the formal system as a member of that class. Gödel's theorem has many implications. In the context of our present speculation, it can be understood primarily as a reconfirmation of the paradox that Cantor revealed. Gödel's demonstration in the incompleteness theorem was developed along the lines of Whitehead and Russell's *Principia Mathematica*. By showing that even typing would collapse when exposed to the incompleteness theorem, Gödel issued a keen challenge to Russell, who had attempted to evade the paradox by logical typing.

Is Gödel's proof, as Morris Kline stated, so desperate for mathematical foundations? I think not. The real developments in mathematics have been made by applied mathematicians, who remain indifferent to foundations as such; indeed, mathematical development has proceeded *irrationally*, as it were.[3] It is thus inaccurate to say that Gödel's proof pushed mathematics to the point of uncertainty. What is more accurate is that it emancipated mathematics from the too heavy burden of certainty that had been unfairly placed upon its shoulders. More to the point, Gödel's proof released mathematics from the illusion of the architectonic and showed that, under the guise of accepting mathematics as normative, the architectonic had always concealed the absence of its own foundation. Despite its solid, if tautological, appearance, mathematics continues even today to develop in manifold ways precisely because it is not an edifice. Mathematics, we can say, is essentially historical.

Author's Note

It has been said that in the Pythagorean school the existence of the irrational number, though known, was taboo. In mathematics the irrational designates something that cannot be described by a *ratio* of natural numbers. For example, a form of a quadratic equation like $X^2 = 2$ cannot exist; rather, it is expressed in the formula $X = 2/X$. X is thus the prerequisite to knowing X. In that case, isn't what the Pythagorean school confronted in the aforementioned equation already the self-referential paradox? A prohibition of the irrational number is in fact equal to the prohibition of self-referentiality. However, in the context of post-Cartesian, modern mathematics, the same equation is described as $X = \sqrt{2}$; and, by treating $\sqrt{2}$ as a number, the paradox is dissolved. Nevertheless, the whole movement of this expansion (invention) of numbers was driven by a series of crises—paradox and solution—and ultimately reached Cantor, who regarded even the infinite as a number and then ended up reencountering the paradox of self-referentiality. But it does not end there. George Spencer-Brown resolved the paradox of self-referentiality by formulating it into another quadratic equation, which Francisco J. Varela used to theorize self-organizing networks. These examples from the current scene, however, neither diminish nor render obsolete the importance of Gödel's proof—I mention them only to show that mathematics is constantly being invented by shifts of concept.

Part Two Becoming

Gödel's proof plays a significant role in this present study because he introduced natural numbers as numbers that are self-referential. Likewise, the process of formalizing natural language makes us aware that the attempt to do so is itself made possible by natural language. To reiterate a point made earlier, natural language and *natural* numbers are not natural, but "what nature makes." Matters to which we provisionally apply the adjective "natural," then, are neither contradictory to the artificial nor distinct from it. Rather, they are part of "what man makes," though the procedure by which they are made is not known, or, more gravely, the "natural" itself is what makes human.

As opposed to the program of general semiology, to which Saussure's general linguistics ostensibly belongs, Roland Barthes insisted on the primacy of linguistics, for as he noted, a general semiology is made possible by language. Saussure was aware of the danger and the ultimate impossibility of "solving" the reciprocal nature of the relationship between general semiology and linguistics. In one place in his *Course in General Linguistics* Saussure stated that linguistics is a part of general semiology, while in another place he stated that general semiology is a part of linguistics. It is a contradiction that Saussure either chose not to solve or found too difficult.

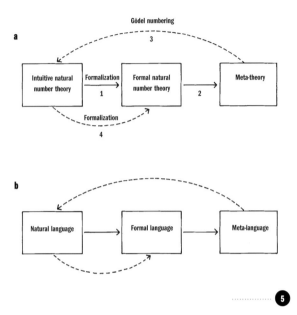

If natural language is inserted in the place of the natural numbers in figure 5a, the result (figure 5b) is a cyclical structure that proves that even if natural language is formalized—reduced to certain symbols—the interpretation or definition of the symbolic form must be executed by natural language itself. The whole scheme presents not only the impossibility of metalanguage, but also the impossibility of natural language as a foundation. Accordingly, we can say that natural language is itself this loop.

Language is essentially a language about language; it is not simply a differential (formal) system, but a self-referential, self-relational system—a system that is differential to itself. A self-referential formal system—or a self-differential differential system—is devoid of both base and center; it is multicentered and excessive. The conceptual framework of Saussure's *langue* is based therefore on the prohibition of such self-referentiality, and yet it is unable to refrain from self-referentiality.

It is possible that in the midst of his attempt to formalize language Saussure became aware of its impossibility. This received attention later in the context of the poststructuralist critique of structuralism, especially with respect to Saussure's strange obsession with the anagram: in private he attempted to prove that all the classic, Western literary works have an anagrammatic structure that conveys another set of meanings. This personal quest was later formally generalized by Julia Kristeva and the Tel Quel group, who claimed that every text produced an alternative to the determined signification. The crucial point here is that natural language is itself a cyclical drive and that whenever formalized, it produces a self-referential paradox.

If formalized, the attempt to push a textual signification to the point of undecidability by locating another, apparently counter signification within the same text results in Gödel's proof. This, however, does not privilege Gödel or mathematics, because formalization as such did not derive from mathematics itself, but from the *will to architecture* that was imposed upon mathematics. Yet this *formalization* is useful in order to deprivilege the somewhat esoteric discourses of poststructuralism.

Texts contain contradictory significations neither because their true meanings are hidden under the surface in some "deep structure" nor because their meanings are by nature ambiguous. Rather, textual signification will remain undecidable when approached formalistically. For this reason deconstruction does not come about as a result of the forcible extraction of a new set of meanings from the text. Again, with Gödel's proof formal systems are incomplete only insofar as they are consistent. In the same way, the deconstructive reading of a text is possible only under the condition that the explicit meaning of a text is literally accepted at least once. Deconstruction is thus not another name for arbitrary interpretation.

On the rapport between deconstruction and the text, de Man maintains that "deconstruction is not something we have added to the text but it constituted the text in the first place."[1] This deconstructive "text," however, is exposed only as a result of our practice of reducing text to structure, and because it is the natural text, namely, the self-referential formal system itself, this attempt to reduce it to a stable form or structure inevitably results in undecidability. This paradoxical mechanism, nevertheless, is not attributable only to the text, but is applicable to all formal systems. One might figuratively call this whole faculty *text*, but doing so in no way returns us to the romanticist fallacy of literature's primacy.

It is now possible for us to reread Karl Marx's *Capital* from a formalist standpoint. Marx begins the first chapter of *Capital* with the following passage: "The wealth of societies in which the capitalist mode of production prevails appears as *an immense 'collection' of commodities [ungeheure Waarensammlung]*; the individual commodity appears as its elementary 'form.' Our investigation therefore begins with the 'analysis' of the commodity."[1] To proceed formally, we must read the terms in italics as if they were written in a mathematical language. Doing so, we can say that Marx reduced preexistent classical economics to *ungeheure Waarensammlung*, to a set that aggregates individual commodities as elements. The form of relations between commodities can thus be grasped as the "form of value." Let us follow Marx's logical deployment.

He begins by extracting the "simple, isolated, or accidental form of value." Marx does not assume this to be an origin from which the "total or expanded form of value" will later develop. This movement should be interpreted neither as a historical development nor a development in the sense of Hegelian dialectics. What is noteworthy about the "simple, isolated, or accidental form of value" is described by Marx:

The value of the linen can therefore only be expressed relatively, i.e. in another commodity. The relative form of value of the linen therefore presupposes that some other commodity confronts it in the equivalent form. On the other hand, this other commodity, which figures as the equivalent, cannot simultaneously be in the relative form of value. It is not the latter commodity whose value is being expressed. It only provides the material in which the value of the first commodity is expressed.

Of course, the expression 20 yards of linen = 1 coat, or 20 yards of linen are worth 1 coat, also includes its converse: 1 coat = 20 yards of linen, or 1 coat is worth 20 yards of linen. But in this case I must reverse the equation, in order to express the value of the coat relatively; and, if I do that, the linen becomes the equivalent instead of the coat.[2]

Likewise, the expression "The value of the linen is expressed by the use-value of the coat" can be reversed to "The value of the coat is expressed by the use-value of the linen." What is crucial here is this "reversibility," which Marx explains figuratively as the relationship between "king and subjects." In other words, in such a form of value it is indeterminable which commodity becomes the figure (positive) and which commodity becomes the ground (negative). No sooner is this reversibility prohibited, and a single commodity surfaces out of a multitude to monopolize the position of the equivalent form, than every other commodity (sign) begins to obtain individual value.

Keeping this in mind, let us look at "the total or expanded form of value":

Z quantity of A commodity = U quantity of B commodity

Z quantity of A commodity = V quantity of C commodity

Z quantity of A commodity = W quantity of D
commodity

Z quantity of A commodity = X quantity of E
commodity.

Since this relationship is reversible, any commodity can
replace A. In this context, the relational system of commodities (signs) is neither simply a unidirectional, infinite chain nor a "relational system devoid of center." It
is better described as a relational system in which innumerable centers coexist, none of which can be considered primary. Marx writes of the "defects" of this phase
of value form:

Firstly, the relative expression of value of the commodity is
incomplete, because the series of its representations never
comes to an end. The chain, of which each equation of value is
a link, is liable at any moment to be lengthened by a newly created commodity, which will provide the material for a fresh
expression of value.[3]

Here Marx is discussing the general form of value or the
money form—the advent of the commodity as a transcendental center—as if it were a logical necessity.
However, the order of this description is inverted,
because the very world that was completed by the general form of value or the money form—upon which the
classical school of economics operated—was nothing
other than an effect of the centralization of the "total or
expanded form of value," as it were, of the rhizomatic
polysystem.

In the first edition of *Capital* Marx describes the
advent of the general form of value in an astounding
manner.[4] In this first edition—as opposed to the many
later revisions of *Capital*, all of which are somewhat

Hegelian because of their clean-cut editing and arrangement—something remarkable arises. With respect to the advent of the general equivalent—a commodity that occupies exclusively the position of the equivalent form—Marx identifies a paradox in which a class of the meta-level descends to the object level to occupy the same locus as the members; in other words, to become a member of itself.

In the phase of the "relative form of value," every commodity (sign) can potentially occupy the meta-level, while the transcendental center that consolidates the system is absent. Nevertheless, the logical typing cannot be completed even in the phase of the "money form." Strangely enough, at the same time as it is standing on the meta-level and therefore closing the "relational system" of commodity, money (*qua* commodity) descends, on its own accord, to the object level. The theory of the value form cannot conclude with the becoming of money. It is instead consummated when the becoming of money is transgressed. It is this very "disequilibrium" that provides the essentially deconstructive disposition of capitalism.

Why is Marx's paradox of the money form inevitable? On account of capital itself, which, though bought and sold as stock, is included among the set of commodities mentioned at the beginning of this chapter. Like Cantor, who treated infinity as a number, Marx developed his "theory of sets" by treating capital itself, and therefore money itself, as a commodity. It was thus not the *generality* but the *infinity* of money that interested Marx. Money must not be regarded as a general measure of value, but rather as a commodity that is unconditionally exchangeable.

Classical economics ignores this aspect of money by defining money as a barometer that indicates the magnitude of value. By excluding money, the classical schools of economics were able to achieve an equilibrate system. The same can be said for the neoclassical school and, for that matter, most Marxian economists. On the other hand, Marx stresses that such an equilibrium is essentially nonexistent. It is therefore absolutely impossible to control capitalism from the meta-level, because capitalism itself is deconstructive.

This does not mean that *Capital* can be reduced to this interpretation. What I would like to say here is that Marx was experiencing the same crisis that has accompanied formalization since the latter half of the nineteenth century; having written the "foundations" of economics, Marx simultaneously realized—sooner than anyone else—the absence of its foundation.

Communication is usually understood as a model in which an ideal speaker and an ideal listener exchange messages by means of a common code. This model is isomorphic to the model of classical and neoclassical economics. The equilibrium theory of classical economics, especially that of Vilfredo Pareto, could not have been very far from Saussure's thoughts when he produced his synchronic system. Many if not most of Saussure's figurative expressions have their roots in economics, and were drawn from work prior to Marx's critique. Figuratively speaking, Saussure's linguistic model could be likened to that system which excludes money, to use the economic term, and to that which excludes the "social hieroglyphic," to use Marx's term. As Derrida might say, Saussure's system excluded *écriture*. As long as we assume this, as did Jakobson and Lévi-Strauss, we have no choice but to assume a "cold structure" with a stable equilibrium.

There are critical movements, however, that attempt to introduce dynamism into this static structure; the introduction of *parole* as against *langue* in linguistics, for example, or, in the more general context, the introduction of an exterior to the system. When this occurs, statements such as "the dialectical reciprocation between a system and its exteriority" become dominant. This way of thinking exhibits a complete ignorance of formalization. Even though Saussure used examples from national languages such as French and English, his *langue* is clearly distinct from those actual languages. By introducing the concept of *langue* Saussure sought to deny the language that is an ideological apparatus in the service of modern nation-states. *Langue* was originally discovered as a differential system that would distinguish the senses, individually, so long as they already existed for the subject. For that very reason, and from the outset, it was impossible to make *langue* "dynamic."

However, as we have already seen, Saussure was not a structuralist in a strict sense. He became aware of the mysterious loop during his exercise of formalizing language, a loop caused by the self-referential nature of language—the fact that language is a language about language. Language is originally dynamic because it is self-referential, and thus there is no need to introduce an exterior to make it so. Furthermore there is no exterior of language—as Derrida stated, there is no *hors-d'oeuvre* of text. Of course, this is true only to the extent that one sees text as a self-referential formal system.

Perhaps the only person in the field of linguistics who can be identified as a pure structuralist is Jakobson. Both Jakobson and Lévi-Strauss relied on a notion of structure derived from Bourbaki. For Bourbaki structure meant the relation between elements within a set comprising three categories—algebraic structures, structures of order, and topological structures. Since these are all constructed by avoiding the paradox of the theory of sets (the self-referential paradox), the structure automatically becomes static and closed even though it is accompanied by a transformational operation. As we have already seen, any attempt to make structure dynamic by direct means is fruitless. However, if the self-referential paradox is introduced, all of these structures—algebraic, topological, and structures of order—are transformed. We can call this attribute the "self-referential formal system."

We must now look at this "self-referential formal system" in the context of communication. Natural communication is far more complex than semiologists usually understand it to be. De Man offers this example from the mass media: When Archie Bunker, the well-known sitcom character from the 1970s, is asked by his wife Edith whether he wants to have his bowling shoes laced over or under, he answers with the question, "What's the difference?" His wife replies by patiently explaining the difference. Even though he meant, "I don't give a damn what the difference is," his wife understood it as a question about the difference between lacing over and lacing under. De Man uses this as an example to suggest that the same grammatical pattern engenders two mutually exclusive meanings.[1] At least within formalism it is impossible to decide whether this sentence is questioning or refusing questioning itself.

Our ability to laugh at the undecidability of the sitcom implies that we stand on a meta-level. A more serious situation is witnessed with schizophrenics, whose lives are conditioned by undecidability. Gregory Bateson elaborates on this in *Steps to an Ecology of Mind*:

Although in formal logic there is an attempt to maintain this discontinuity between a class and its members, we argue that in the psychology of real communications this discontinuity is continually and inevitably breached, and that a priori we must expect a pathology to occur in the human organism when certain formal patterns of the breaching occur in the communication between mother and child. We shall argue that this pathology at its extreme will have symptoms whose formal characteristics would lead the pathology to be classified as a schizophrenia.[2]

In Zen Buddhism there is a style of teaching in which the master holds a stick over the pupil's head and says fiercely, "If you say this stick is real, I will strike you with it. If you say this stick is not real, I will strike you with it. If you don't say anything, I will strike you with it." Bateson calls such a situation the double bind. With Zen, the pupil chooses to be in this undecidable situation; moreover, the student might even reach up and snatch the stick away from the master, who could accept such an action as *satya*. The interrogations of Zen are always embellished by this kind of subtly cruel but comical factor that is enabled precisely by the possibility of standing on a meta-level.

   Schizophrenics constantly find themselves in situations like that of the pupil. But for them, there is no escape. Bateson offers a few examples, including the following, which is related to the family situation. While physically punishing a child, a mother sends verbal messages such as "Do not see it as punishment," "Do not obey my order," or "Do not think about what you should not do." It should be obvious that these are self-referential sentences and are thus undecidable. Situations like the double bind are formed by contradictory messages between the levels of nonverbal communication (posture, gesture, and tone of voice) and verbal communication. Another example occurs when the father denies what the mother has already ordered the child to do. When two different levels (types) of messages are sent from one side, and they are contradictory, the intended recipient of the message will be trapped in the double bind. The double bind, then, always occurs in a self-referential, and therefore undecidable, system.

As Bateson stresses, the repetition of such double bind experiences in family situations is necessary to the development of the schizophrenic pathology in children. According to Bateson, those who grow up in repetitively enforced double bind situations, where communication and meta-communication are incompatible, cannot distinguish logical types. This condition, however, occurs not only in schizophrenics but in everyone. When someone is confronted with mutually conflicting messages on two different levels and is unable but required to comment on the contradictions, the same sense of disorientation occurs, as Bateson observes in this example: "For example, one day an employee went home during office hours. A fellow employee called him at his home, and said lightly, 'Well, how did you get *there*?' The employee replied, 'By automobile.' He responded literally.[3] A schizophrenic confounds a literal message and a metaphorical message in the same way; when someone is joking, he or she understands it literally and responds defensively.

Shifting the mode of expression from the literal to the metaphorical usually helps resolve the double bind. However, if the person is unaware that the message is metaphorical, a pathology is engendered. Furthermore, with schizophrenics, communication about communication—the meta-communicative system—is collapsed, and the types of messages are confused. Schizophrenics are unable to understand what the messages sent really mean, tend to become obsessed with what they imagine is a "hidden meaning," and set out to prove that they will never be tricked. Another response is to receive every message literally and reject all meta-communication. Yet another response is to ignore everything in an attempt to avoid situations that require responses. In this latter situation, the person ends up abandoning all interest in the outside. One might say that each of these behavioral patterns corresponds to a mode and stage of schizophrenia.

Schizophrenia, after all, occurs when the type categorization of the formal system, which is originally self-referential, is destroyed. In psychoanalysis, this typing—the prohibition of self-referentiality—is called castration or foreclosure. Moreover, it is this prohibition that constitutes the formal system (the Symbolic order in Lacanian analysis); however, the Symbolic order is essentially ungrounded—it is riddled with holes that cannot be filled. According to Jacques Lacan, the failure of the foreclosure or symbolic castration induces psychosis. Psychotics live, as it were, within the self-referential paradox.

My intention is not to connect Lacan and Bateson. Bateson's critique of Russell by way of the "psychology of communication" shows that Bateson was unwittingly confronting the Gödelian problematic. Bateson's analysis of schizophrenia is provocative for two reasons. First, far from the conventional phenomenological accounts of schizophrenia, he shows that the behavior of schizophrenics is organized as a strategy to confront the double bind in communication. Second, he points out that the communication between doctor and patient forms a double bind. Psychoanalytic therapy should position itself to use such situations positively rather than avoiding them. The central or pivotal problematic faced by Lacanian analysis is linked to the same point: not only is the analysand being analyzed by the analyst, but the relationship between analyst and analysand must also be analyzed. To extend the point, this meta-analysis never ends, resulting in interminable analysis. What Lacan attempted to formalize in his discussion of the Möbius strip and other mathematical figures need not be restricted to psychoanalysis precisely because it is formalized—I myself do not acknowledge the necessity to participate in such esoteric language games.

In criticizing the Lacanian school, Gilles Deleuze and Félix Guattari affirm schizophrenia. The rhizome that they posit as an alternative to the tree, however, is a *radicalization* of Alexander's semi-lattice.[4] No matter how complex and manifold it may seem, the semi-lattice, as developed by Alexander, is a compound created from two or more trees. Despite its appearance, it is orderly and centered. The semi-lattice thus hides the transcendental *cogito*. In spite of the fact that it accommodates overlapping and indeterminacy, it is based upon the law of contradiction (this or that) or upon the distinction of class and member (logical types). What happens then, when the semi-lattice is broken? Both "this and that" are realized; transverse communication between categories occurs incessantly, and multiple centers (on the meta-level) are simultaneously established as a result of the dissolution of logical type. If the tree and the semi-lattice can be seen to correspond to the structures of order in a set, Deleuze and Guattari's rhizome comes into play when the paradox of the theory of sets is introduced to the structures. We might say that the rhizome is akin to what Bateson calls schismogenesis. Indeed, the rhizome is modeled after the cerebral nerve center—natural intelligence is taken into account. Yet, as we have seen, we can approach natural intelligence only by the "making" of artificial intelligence, and by its impossibility—which we have already witnessed in Gödel's proof. We can now see, then, that many of the problems that we have been discussing are problems of formalization.

Jane Jacobs views the limitations of city planning in a way different from Alexander. First of all she audaciously asserts, "Cities first—rural development later,"[1] against the idea that the development of agriculture or rural villages gave rise to cities, an idea that has been dominant since Adam Smith. Jacobs's thesis is not about the historical order of development: for her, the city is not a form that has existed substantially, but the formal attribute of "cityness" that characterizes a city as long as it is a city.

For Jacobs, cities name the development of the division of labor that is caused by the addition of new work to old work. New work is always produced by *combining* one's own work with some other kind of work. She writes, "The point is that when new work is added to older work, the addition often cuts ruthlessly across categories of work, no matter how one may analyze the categories. Only in stagnant economies does work stay docilely within given categories."[2]

Jacobs says that when D (the division of labor of a work) is added to A (a new activity), increase (diversification) occurs; it is formulated as $D + A = nD$ and its diversification is illustrated in figure 6.[3] She analyzes the "logic" of this event as follows:

To be sure, the process is full of surprises and is hard to predict—possibly it is unpredictable—before it has happened. But after the fact, after the added goods or services exist, their addition usually looks wonderfully logical and "natural."

What kind of logic is this? It is analogous, I think, to a form of logic, or intuition if you prefer, that artists use.[4]

There is no doubt that this type of logic is isomorphic to that found in natural intelligence. We might say then that if Alexander, as a kind of structuralist, sees the natural city as a semi-lattice, then Jacobs grasps it as a rhizome. According to her, city planning and economic planning in general invariably arrange—from the position of a transcendent center—components into a *logical* tree structure. The living city—a development of the division of labor—on the other hand, is engendered by multiple centers and, simultaneously, by the "unpredictable crossing of categories." This is why "premeditated" city planning—whether executed by bourgeoisie or Marxists—necessarily fails. Rather than relying on enormous amounts of calculated investment or centralized plans designed by civic leaders, Jacobs insists that the only way to intervene in the formation of cities is to accelerate the differentiation in the disoriented and *naturwüchsige* networks.

Her extensive citation of historical fact notwithstanding, Jacobs's tactics are no less formalist than

Alexander's. Her "embryonic city" cannot be proven true by archaeological data, nor can it be inferred through an observation of uncivilized societies because, unlike existing uncivilized societies, which are structurally stable and equilibrate systems, it is essentially disequilibrate, excessive, and disorientedly open. The embryonic city exists not only primordially but presently, whereas uncivilized societies have formed their static structure by closing schismogenesis, by deliberately or accidentally isolating themselves in each stage of development. In short, the embryonic city as such *exists* only *formally*, rather than factually or historiographically.

Jacobs privileges the city over agriculture because the city acknowledges the self-differential differential system as a formal precedent. We must thus take into account her formalization of three concepts—city, town, and village—though they do not correspond to the commonly understood divisions of progressively greater scale. "City" designates a state of development, while "town" designates a stagnated state of differentiation. Cities such as Detroit or Pittsburgh are already "towns" according to Jacobs's ahistorical and formal categorization. Interestingly enough, this division of village, town, and city corresponds to Deleuze and Guattari's three-part division of coding, decoding, and overcoding. Since none of these are historical concepts—they can exist in any historical phase—we can say that the planned city or economy is a town par excellence.

Jacobs writes, "In just such ways, I think, our understanding of cities, and also of economic development generally, has been distorted by the dogma of agricultural primacy."[5] She goes on to say that even Marx was affected by Adam Smith's dogma. It was Smith, after all, who attached such importance to the division of labor, from which he formulated his model of general social history. Since Smith focused not on the previous class structure or caste society but instead on the factory or the specialization in the factory that came into existence during the industrial revolution in England, he saw the previous society as a system of the division of labor. Therefore it was the specialization within the factory that enabled him to see society as a transformation of the differential system, and *not vice versa*. The previous society thus did not develop teleologically into the more advanced complex division of labor.

Here we can see the emergence of the transcendent viewpoint that assumes a view of the whole process of social history, a view from which it can then plan the development of a whole society. When this transcendent view looks to the past, the history of the origin becomes the most important feature of the history it writes. In this way, the historicity of the factory or specialization in the factory is structurally neglected or forgotten. Ecological recognition originally occurred as a result of the application of this Smithian notion of the division of labor to the field of biology. It is the double oblivion and fabrication of the origin—by the ecologists—that sets nature's harmonious ecosystem against industrial development.

As Jacobs claims, many so-called Marxists accept an unexamined version of the Smithian notion of the "division of labor." Engels, for example, writes:

But where, in a given society, the fundamental form of production is that spontaneous division of labor which creeps in gradually and not upon any preconceived plan, there the products take on the form of *commodities*, whose mutual exchange, buying and selling, enable the individual producers to satisfy their manifold wants. And this was the case in the Middle Ages. The peasant, e.g., sold to the artisan agricultural products and bought from him the products of handicraft. Into this society of individual producers, of commodity producers, the new mode of production thrust itself. In the midst of the old division of labor, grown up spontaneously and upon *no definite plan*, which had governed the whole of society, now arose division of labor upon a *definite plan*, as organized in the factory; side by side with *individual* production appeared *social* production.[6]

For Engels, socialism is, first and foremost, the control of *Naturwüchsigkeit*, or the anarchic drive of a society. It should not be surprising that Lenin's idea of turning society into "a gigantic factory" derived from this understanding.[7] Marx, however, proceeds along a completely different line. In *Capital* Marx stresses the importance of manufacturing rather than that of the factory or machine. As Lewis Mumford noted, the notion of the factory and factory organization came from the army or temple, and thus its organizational system is that of the tree.

According to Marx, the development of the division of labor in manufacturing is a *contingent* process in which the differentiation of the same and the transverse connection of difference are constantly occurring. Manufacturing came into existence as a rearrangement of the various elements of handicraft, which until then had been fixed by the guilds. Manufacturing first appeared as a deconstruction of the overcoded medieval communities; but as soon as it became "factory," it was reappropriated. Specialization (division of labor) appeared as though it had been planned from the beginning.

There is a certain correspondence between the priority of manufacturing over the factory that Marx writes about and the priority of the city over the rural village that Jacobs calls for. It is important to note that Marx revealed the secret of capital development from a non-historical, genealogical problematic. He saw it as lying in "manufacturing" rather than in the "factory," and he revealed the inversion that fabricated a necessity in an accidental event such as the establishment of the factory.

Engels consistently opposed the unchecked forces of *Naturwüchsigkeit*, while Marx affirmed them. In *The German Ideology*, Marx reiterated the terms "division of labor" and "intercourse," which Engels later replaced with "forces and relations of production." In Marx's terminology, specialization (division of labor) amounts to differentiation, while intercourse amounts to a hybridization of specialization or differentiation. As expressed in his statement "war itself is . . . a regular form of intercourse,"[8] Marx's concept of intercourse is more nuanced, accommodating the accidental, the ungrounded, the transverse, the erotic, and the violent, while Engels's concept of "relations of production" is an enclosed system of relation.

In *The German Ideology*, Marx developed this account of the division of labor (differentiation) and intercourse (accidental and transverse connection) and not, as many assume, an account of the "precedence of agriculture." These concepts, coming as they did after Hegel, were developed in order to *invert* those aspects of Hegel's thought that asserted a view of history as "making" and *Geist* as a maker of that world history. Because originally written as a critique of Ludwig Feuerbach, who already had "inverted" Hegelian idealism, these terms neither explain history as a narrative of dialectical materialism nor are they simply the materialistic inversion of Hegelian idealism. Contrary to Hegel's view of history, Marx saw history as "natural history." Men and women do make history, but there is no true maker or subject in the process of this event; even though made by men and women, the process of history's making or semi-becoming will never be transparent, and will always be obscure. Marx therefore attempted to detail the workings of a certain human force that works to bring about such events. In this context, *Naturwüchsigkeit* is pivotal.

> The social power, i.e. the multiplied productive force, which arises through the co-operation of different individuals as it is determined by the division of labor, appears to these individuals, since their cooperation is not voluntary but has come about naturally [*Naturwüchsigkeit*], not as their own unified power, but as an alien force existing outside them, of the origin and goal of which they are ignorant, which they thus cannot control, which on the contrary passes through a peculiar series of phases and stages independent of the will and the action of man, nay even being the prime governor of these.[9]

Marx did not believe that *Naturwüchsigkeit* would ultimately be controllable. In contrast to Engels, who envisioned progress from the "kingdom of nature" to the "kingdom of freedom," Marx unfolded the primordiality of becoming through making, and this is distilled in this word *Naturwüchsigkeit*. Within Marxism, the Engels-Lenin lineage denied *Naturwüchsigkeit* as bourgeois and anarchic, whereas Rosa Luxemburg affirmed it and thought that "consciousness of purpose" must amend itself through an incessant dialogue or dialectic with *Naturwüchsigkeit*. In her view the organizational theory of the party made it impossible to recognize the implications of *Naturwüchsigkeit*. In fact, Luxemburg preferred the term *Spontaneität* to *Naturwüchsigkeit*—despite the fact that Marx himself had consistently used the latter throughout *Capital*. The concept of *Spontaneität* originated in deism, while *Naturwüchsigkeit* contains the image of flora propagating, just as with Deleuze and

Guattari's rhizome. By promoting *Naturwüchsigkeit*, Marx was pointing to something from which the opposition between *Naturwüchsigkeit* and consciousness of purpose derives, the same distinction Jacobs set forth with respect to cities.

Furthermore, seen from the point of view of "division of labor" and "intercourse," history is devoid of both Hegelian "reason" and a Eurocentric center; it has no beginning and no end (*telos*). Because "division of labor" and "intercourse"—history as differentiation and as transverse connection—are, in essence, accidental and nonsensical, approaches that insist on reason and center must be recognized as ideological. What is the origin of the ideology that fabricates these into a linear, historical progression whose endpoint is the tree structure?

With these there develops the division of labor, which was originally nothing but the division of labor in the sexual act, then that division of labor which develops spontaneously or "naturally" [*Naturwüchsigkeit*] by virtue of natural predisposition (e.g. physical strength), needs, accidents, etc., etc. Division of labor only becomes truly such from the moment when a division of material and mental labor appears. (The first form of ideologists, *priests*, is concurrent.) From this moment onwards consciousness *can* really flatter itself that it is something other than consciousness of existing practice, that it *really* represents something without representing real; from now on consciousness is in a position to emancipate itself from the world and to proceed to the formation of 'pure' theory, theology, philosophy, ethics, etc.[10]

Here Marx is not saying that the state of *naturwüchsiges* division of labor had been dominant until a certain phase of history, after which the "true division of labor" became dominant; what is implied, instead, is that as the *naturwüchsiges* state of division of labor emerges, at a certain point a power intervenes—a power that incessantly attempts to administrate and suppress from above. This is not just ancient history. In fact, Marx later in this text talks about the same mechanism a propos the development from manufacturing to factory.

In the same paragraph Marx also addresses the origin of the architect as metaphor (the philosopher). He asks "Who talks?" rather than "What is talked about?" The Hegelian *Geist* and the narrative account of history are themselves products of the division of labor, products of a consciousness (philosopher) that, by the grace of the division of labor, was enabled to think itself autonomous. Whether they like it or not, philosophers are constantly driven by a structure or force that is manifest as *naturwüchsiges*, yet they always represent the result of its differentiality as contradiction. As a result, contradiction is regarded as the motivating force, the motor of history.

Class struggle understood as the motor of history is a fiction, even though the class struggle itself is undeniable. As Jacobs writes, "The conflict between the process of adding new work to old and the guilds' categories of work was a constant source of wrangling in medieval European cities."[11] This same struggle exists today, and will certainly continue into the future. For Marx the class struggle is always observed within the context of cities and in the form of discourses; it has always existed, but only as a struggle between action—which incessantly differentiates itself *nonorientedly* by way of the "unpredictable surprise attack"—and reaction—which attempts to restrict such action to the preexisting stable system. The Marxian class struggle, therefore, is not something that exists substantively; instead it can only be illuminated by an ex post facto reading, in the way, for example, that Nietzsche interpreted religion and philosophy in terms of a "class struggle" (by means of the figures of warrior and priest). The class struggle exists neither in the form of binary opposition nor in the contradiction between capitalist and proletariat. Such oppositions are ideologies that reduce and simplify the actual mode of the ever-becoming, ever-transforming division of labor and intercourse. Class struggle is a fiction that explains history as a *becoming-by-contradiction* and that suppresses the many class struggles that in fact are the becomings of the manifold. Class struggle is thus possible only as a struggle against such a narrative itself.

Author's Note

A. F. Hayek calls the sort of thought that conceives of a whole society as transparently comprehensible and designable "constructivism," and he identifies Marx and Descartes as the progenitors of this position. This is a vulgar simplification. I will address this view of Descartes later, but I would like to say a word about Marx here. Hayek opposed constructivism to "spontaneous order." This seems to be similar, in a sense, to the *Naturwüchsigkeit* that Marx posed against Hegelianism.

It is noteworthy that Marx deliberately avoided *Spontaneität* because of its deistic implications and instead used *Naturwüchsigkeit*. The nuances inherent in this difference, however, are lost in the translation from German to English. The former term implies that, *by the grace of God*, the spontaneous will of an individual will result in an order of preestablished harmony. Hayek's notion of spontaneous order conspicuously includes an assumption by Adam Smith that the "invisible hand [of God]" controls the market economy. For that reason, Hayek later replaced spontaneous order with "self-organizing system," though of course the latter is also a *system*. The anarchists in Marx's time also considered "spontaneity" to be important—which is not in the least contradictory to the fact that they wished to design utopia (Charles Fourier and Pierre Joseph Proudhon). Herein resides a deism commonly shared with classical economics and classical liberalism. In striking contrast, Marx denied constructivism altogether and unequivocally refused to speak of a future; thus Marx's opposition to anarchists by no means suggests that he was an "archist." In fact, he supported the Paris Commune, which was led by Proudhonists. What forced the gradual phasing out of anarchism was the expansion of Prussia's state capitalism and its corresponding social democracy.

What Marx attempted to expose by *Naturwüchsigkeit* is the schismogenesis that underlies the polarity between the spontaneous order and the constructive order. As described in this chapter, this schismogenesis cannot be administered by any planned organization; in fact it dissolves orders that are constituted upon the notion of a preestablished harmony. In the context of economics, this indicates that the currency economy immanently embraces disequilibrium; for this reason, centralized economic planning and Keynesian intervention are inexorably invoked. However, Marx's thesis does not conclude in this way. *Capital* is, first and foremost, a Kantian "critique" of "national economics"; it reveals that both constructivism and spontaneous order—forming thesis and antithesis— are merely a semblance (*Schein*).

The self-referential formal system is dynamic because of incessant internal slippage (self-differentiation). It cannot maintain a definitive meta-level or center that systematizes a system. Rather, like the "multiplicity of subjects" that Nietzsche once proposed, it is multicentered.[1] Because, as the intuitionists observed, the law of the excluded middle cannot be established in these conditions, the necessity of choosing "*either* this or that" is replaced by "*both* this and that." In short, the self-referential formal system is always dis-   *Eleven* **Being** equilibrate and excessive.

Structuralists attempted to construct an equilibrate system precisely by suppressing self-referentiality. Yet those who applied mathematical structuralism to their own fields of study encountered the same aporia that mathematical structuralism had encountered—one thinks for example of the gaps that structure the Lacanian Symbolic. But rather than focusing on Lacan we turn to the work of Lévi-Strauss, where a certain instability—compelled by the very objects of his research—is omnipresent.

Lévi-Strauss understood the elementary structure of kinship in uncivilized societies—which appears to be disordered from the empirical view—as a formal structure. He managed to see as identical forms that were seemingly diversified according to region. Because he had chosen the structure of kinship as his object of analysis, Lévi-Strauss had to deal with the origin of the prohibition of incest, the very structure that makes the kinship system possible. Lévi-Strauss treated the prohibition of incest not from the genetic viewpoint, but as a logical sine qua non for the existence of a formal structure. The prohibition of incest thus became the prohibition of self-referentiality.

No one previous to Lévi-Strauss had proceeded along this line of inquiry. Indeed, the prohibition of incest had been interpreted mostly from the standpoint of either psychologism or functionalism. It was necessary for Lévi-Strauss to reject these views, for his entire project was dependent on formalizing the various forms of kinship. In his approach the prohibition of incest is less a historical or genetic problematic than a logical given that is necessary in order to comprehend the formal system.

Though it appears that Lévi-Strauss raises the issue of the "origin" of the prohibition of incest *genetically*, he is in fact doing just the opposite. His approach is not unlike that of Husserl, who, in his search for the "origin of geometry," had not approached the question from a historicist viewpoint, despite appearances to the contrary. In fact, as Lévi-Strauss stressed, extant "uncivilized" societies have nothing to do with primitive societies in a historiographical sense, and therefore historical origin is in no way illuminated by an examination of an uncivilized society. But neither can we depend on the archaeological corpora, mythology, and folklore. The only acceptable approaches are either formal or retrospective. In his retrospective approach, Lévi-Strauss encountered *an unstable shaking* in the very foundation upon which structuralism would later construct its stable formal system.

Lévi-Strauss gives the name culture to intersubjective forms such as language and custom. It should be obvious that no culture or social system originates in nature. If we do not consider culture as an a priori given, it can only be deduced from nature. But culture does not emerge from nature. Lévi-Strauss solved this by turning to "prohibition."

We have shown that each of the early theoreticians who tackled the problem of the incest prohibition held one of the three following points of view. Some put forward the natural and cultural duality of the rule, but could only establish a rationally derived and extrinsic connection between the two aspects. Others have explained the prohibition of incest solely or predominantly if not in terms of natural causes, then as a cultural phenomenon. Each of these three outlooks has been found to lead to impossibilities or contradictions. Consequently, a tradition from static analysis to dynamic synthesis is the only path remaining open. The prohibition of incest is in origin neither purely cultural nor purely natural, nor is it a composite mixture of elements from both nature and culture. It is the fundamental step because of which, by which, but above all in which, the transition from nature to culture is accomplished. In one sense, it belongs to nature, for it is a general condition of culture. Consequently, we should not be surprised that its formal characteristic, universally, has been taken from nature. However, in another sense, it is already culture, exercising and imposing its rule on phenomena which initially are not subject to it. WE HAVE BEEN LED to pose the problem of incest in connection with the relationship between man's biological existence and his social existence, and we have immediately established that the prohibition could not be ascribed accurately to either one or the other. In the present work we propose to find the solution to this anomaly by showing that the prohibition of incest is the link between them.[2]

What is at stake here is nothing less than undecidability. The prohibition of incest is "what man makes," but it is not made by man, because it is this prohibition itself that makes man into man. Then who makes it? Lévi-Strauss maintains that "the prohibition of incest is where nature transcends itself."[3] But even as he announces this, Lévi-Strauss's sense of nature is being transformed—it is no longer the sort of nature that opposes culture. This question arises if, and only if, one attempts to construct a formal structure. It is a question that Lévi-Strauss did not struggle with for very long.

I cannot help but connect this with Martin Heidegger's question, What is the difference between beings and Being? Analytic philosophers have ridiculed this as a question of differentiation between object and meta-level. Like these philosophers, I do not appreciate Heidegger's parading around of the concept of Being. Instead, in accordance with Nietzsche,[4] whom Heidegger criticized as remaining within the limits of the metaphysics of "forgottenness of Being," I want to suggest that ontology is prescribed by the grammar inherent in Indo-European languages. (As implied earlier, however, Heidegger was acquainted with formalism under the rubric of cybernetics, which Nietzsche of course did not know.) What does the "differentiation between beings and Being" mean in this context?

That relation is revealed as discordant. The question still remains whether the discordancy of our relation to Being lies in us or in Being itself; the answer to that question may once again decide something important about the essence of the relation.

Still more pressing than the question of whether the opposites identified lie in the essence of Being itself, or whether they merely arise out of *our* discordant relation to

Being, *or whether this relation of ours to Being in fact springs from Being itself,* since it abides by Being—more pressing than these indubitably decisive questions is the following: Viewed with respect to matters as they stand, *is* our relation to Being a discordant one? Do we comport ourselves toward Being so discordantly that the discord completely dominates *us;* that is to say, our comportment toward beings? We must answer in the negative. In our comportment, we merely stand on one side of the opposites: Being is for us the emptiest, most universal, most intelligible, most used, most reliable, most forgotten, most said. We scarcely even heed it, and therefore do not know it *as* an opposition to something else.

Being remains something neutral for us, and for that reason we scarcely pay attention to the differentiation of Being and beings, although we establish all our comportment toward beings on the basis of it. But it is not only we today who stand outside that still unexperienced discord of the relation to Being. Such "standing outside" and "not knowing" is characteristic of all metaphysics, since for metaphysics Being necessarily remains the most universal, the most intelligible. In the scope of Being metaphysics ponders only the multifaceted and multilayered universals of various realms of beings.

Throughout the whole history of metaphysics, from the time Plato interpreted the beingness of beings as *idea* up to the time Nietzsche defined Being as value, Being has been self-evidently well preserved as the *a priori* to which man as a rational creature comports himself. Because the relation to Being has, as it were, dissolved in indifference, the *differentiation* of Being and beings also cannot become questionable for metaphysics.[5]

Suppose that the differentiation between "beings and Being" is equal to that between object level and meta-level, as the logicists claimed. For Russell this difference (distinction) is identified with the logical type. In contrast, the difference that Heidegger stresses destroys these kinds of distinctions. Plato interpreted the being-ness of beings as *idea*, which amounts to preserving dis-tinction (typing) as the logicists maintained; this proves, conversely, that the logicists were working within the range of Platonic metaphysics.

Heidegger shows that an attempt to secure a ratio-nal formal system by means of distinction (typing) is an escape from the situation in which distinction is essen-tially impossible. Although he repeatedly reiterates "the ultimate question"—"Still more pressing than the ques-tion of whether the opposites identified lie in the essence of Being itself, or whether they merely arise out of *our* discordant relation to Being, or whether this rela-tion of ours to Beings in fact springs from Being itself"—Heidegger never develops the ultimate answer. What was instead more important for Heidegger was *not* to respond, and thereby to remain within the unde-cidable question.

In the context of these present speculations, we can put it another way: what Heidegger ultimately con-fronts is the self-referential formal system or the self-differential differential system itself. Accordingly, what he calls the "forgottenness of Being" is the forgetting of self-differentiality itself. Heidegger confronted Husserl, who was a logicist, with ungroundedness, as Gödel had confronted the logicist Russell. Heidegger relates this by way of the metaphor of architecture: "And yet Being offers us no ground and no basis—as beings do—to which we can turn, on which we can build, and to which we can cling. Being is the rejection [*Ab-sage*] of the role of such grounding; it renounces all grounding, is abyssal [*ab-gründig*]."[6]

Likewise, one could say that Plato discovered his ground by regarding the "beingness of beings" as *idea*, thereupon constructing the architecture of the formal system. Ungroundedness nonetheless opens itself up because, as Gödel demonstrated, formal systems are destined to result in self-referentiality. We can also state the converse: that Heidegger's "forgottenness" is tantamount to the prohibition of the ungroundedness, undecidability, or self-referentiality that generates excess.

This assessment of Heidegger is itself a formalist one. On the other hand, the political implications of his activities are well-known. This brings us to the question: Can we measure the work of a thinker formally, out of the historical context to which she or he belongs? Again, this is a formalist problem.

Not even philosophy is beyond the reach of formalization. Husserl devoted himself to the question, "What is left for philosophy after formalization?" We might say that if philosophy can be said to exist, it is only in the form of the self-referential question, "What is left for philosophy?" Yet this question itself is not left untouched by formalization.

Today there are calls for philosophy to reconsider its exclusion of rhetoric. In *The Realm of Rhetoric*, Chaim Perelman identifies the "dissociation of ideas" as an argumentative technique that is hardly mentioned in traditional rhetoric. He offers the example appearance/reality, followed by such pairs as accident/essence, relative/absolute, individual/universal, abstract/concrete, act/substance, theory/practice, and so on. He calls the pairing "term I/term II" and explains that these combinations are not diametrically opposed:

With the model of the appearance/reality pair we can present the philosophical pairs in the form of the pair term I/term II.

Term I corresponds to the apparent, to what occurs in the first instance, to what is actual, immediate, and known directly. Term II, to the extent that it is distinguished from it, can be understood only by comparison with term I: it results from a dissociation effected within term I with the purpose of getting rid of the incompatibilities that may appear between different aspects of term I. Term II provides a criterion, a norm which allows us to distinguish those aspects of term I which are of value from those which are not; it is not simply a datum, it is a *construction* which, during the dissociation of term I, establishes a rule that makes it possible to classify the multiple aspects of term I in a hierarchy. It enables those that do not correspond to the rule which *reality* provides to be termed illusory, erroneous, or apparent (in the depreciatory sense of this word). In relation to term I, term II is both normative and explanatory.[1]

Perelman continues by explaining that while the history of Western philosophy operates within such oppositions, "original thought" is engendered by a reversal of the terms of a pair; but it cannot remain simply as a "reversal."

An original thought can quickly bring about a reversal of the terms of a pair. Rarely, however, does this reversal take place without a modification of one or the other term, for it is a matter of pointing out the reasons which justify this reversal. Thus the pair individual/universal, which is characteristic of traditional metaphysics, if reversed, gives the pair abstract/concrete. In fact, the individual, who alone is concrete, is accorded value when the universal is considered not as a superior reality, a Platonic idea, but as an abstraction derived from the concrete. But in this case it is this immediately given which becomes the real, the abstract being only a derivative and theoretical elaboration corresponding to the pair theory/reality.[2]

While term II belongs to the opposition "term I/term II," it is also what sustains the opposition itself; it follows that a reversal cannot be completely accomplished by simply overturning the opposition of term I/term II as the *figure*. Instead, term II itself—as the *ground* on which the opposition itself takes place—must be reversed. In order for that to occur, we must develop conditions in which both figure and ground are, as it were, indeterminable. The logical typing that fixes the hierarchy of term I/term II must be made inoperable.

Derridean deconstruction accomplishes this task. But, we might ask, are not all of the "original" philosophies of the past deconstructive? The fact that they are makes it possible to establish deconstructive readings of them. Changes in philosophy are not prompted only by changed historical circumstances; they also emerge as a result of changes in the very nature of philosophy itself—philosophy is a self-referential system where ultimate determination and closure are impossible. But if this is so, a critique of philosophy results in another dual opposition. The insistence on the superiority of either text or rhetoric over philosophy might become dominant. But is this any different from the previous state of affairs? Is it not, after all, a metaphysics of the text? Derrida addresses this issue as follows:

Whoever alleges that philosophical discourse belongs to the closure of a language must still proceed within this language and with the oppositions it furnishes. According to a law that can be formalized, philosophy always reappropriates for itself the discourse that de-limits it.

In reminding the philosopher that he remains enclosed in a language, Nietzsche was surely more violent and more explicit than anyone else, but he was also exploiting a possibility that had been coming to the surface almost everywhere for a half century, even if most often reappropriated by philosophical interest. In this situation, Nietzschean discourse, no more than any other, could not simply escape the law of reappropriation.[3]

Derrida himself cannot escape this "law." He incessantly shifts his position in order to avoid "reappropriation." Louis Althusser speaks of formalization in the following way:

> The forms and arguments of the fight may vary, but if the whole history of philosophy is merely the history of these forms, they have only to be reduced to the immutable tendencies that they represent for the transformation of these forms to become a kind of *game for nothing*. Ultimately, philosophy has no history; philosophy is that strange theoretical site where nothing really happens, nothing but this *repetition* of nothing.[4]

Both to invert the hierarchy of the dual opposition and to abandon opposition itself, therefore, are formal, nonsensical issues. Yet, as Althusser continues, they are not totally *null*.

> The inversion which is formally the nothing which happens in philosophy, in its explicit discourse, is not null, or rather, it is an effect of annulment, the annulment of a previous hierarchy replaced by the opposite hierarchy. What is at stake in philosophy in the ultimate categories which govern all philosophical systems, is therefore the sense of this hierarchy, the sense of this location of one category in the dominant position.[5]

I must add, however, that this "sense" is not determinable within philosophy. No matter how radical it may be, in some cases the inversion ends up being just another formal game, and in other cases it becomes a dominant ideology before one becomes aware of it. There are certain times and places in which idealism can achieve a revolutionary sense and certain times and places in which materialism can sustain only a reactionary sense. Thus it is impossible to determine the "sense" of philosophy within philosophy, since it can only be determined outside philosophy and outside form. Yet once such an outside is conceptually grasped, it is no longer outside. Here lies the importance of the issue de Man identifies as "formalism as a prison house." Is there any way out?

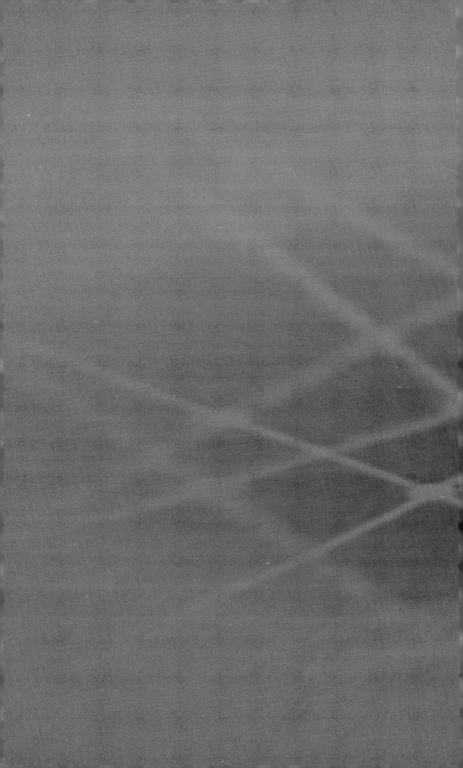

Part Three Teaching and Selling

When it was published in 1931, Gödel's incompleteness theorem had an enormous impact on mathematical and philosophical circles. In the previous
chapters I have attempted to show how this theorem affected other discourses. Now I shall
examine Wittgenstein's important reaction
to Gödel's theorem. During the period in
which he wrote *Philosophical Investigations*
(1936), Wittgenstein appeared to be
indifferent to the uproar that Gödel
had caused. But, as the 1937 publication date of *Remarks on the Foun-
dations of Mathematics* attests, he   *Thirteen* **Solipsism**
did not abandon his interest in
mathematics; indeed, it is hard
to imagine that he could
have avoided altogether
the impact of Gödel's theorem on mathematics.
What is more important,
Philosophical Investigations cannot be understood properly if
these circumstances are not taken
into account. Wittgenstein mentioned Gödel only rarely, and only
then with respect to his critique of
Russell: "It is my task, not to attack
Russell's logic from within, but from without." "My task," he said, "is not to talk about
(e.g.) Gödel's proof, but to by-pass it."[1]

What do these expressions "without" and
"by-pass" mean exactly? That Gödel "attack[s]
Russell's logic from within" clearly delineates the
mechanism by which the incompleteness theorem
operates: it collapses the formal system from within by

drawing out undecidability. In this context the foregoing statements seem to indicate that Wittgenstein replicates Gödel's results, but from "without." Wittgenstein practically ignored Gödel because Gödel's method was confined to the limits set by Russell. More to the point, Wittgenstein believed that Gödel was limited by formalization itself.

Gödel was a tacit Platonist. He revealed the undecidability of Gregor Cantor's continuum hypothesis by claiming that although the error of the hypothesis could not be proven formally, it could be intuited through meditation. Gödel revealed the undecidability of the hypothesis by means of a formal demonstration because he believed in a mathematical reality that would require no further foundation: instead of inscribing it positively, he implied it negatively. We might say then that Wittgenstein was repulsed not so much by Russell but by Gödel's "negative theology," which, under the guise of supporting the formalist foundation, actually deconstructs it. If Gödel's method is related to deconstruction, then Wittgenstein indicates a similar but subtly and *fundamentally* different method.

Referring to Gödel, Wittgenstein claimed, "However queer it sounds, my task as far as concerns Gödel's proof seems merely to consist in making clear what such a proposition as: 'Suppose this could be proved' means in mathematics."[2] Wittgenstein's intention was to radically doubt "proof" itself, a procedure that bypasses the undecidability/decidability division that preoccupied Gödel. Mathematics is considered "solid" only insofar as it is deduced from axioms. But can this be accomplished? Wittgenstein emphasizes that the proof cannot be assumed automatically but only by participants who obey the rules.

Plato extended the geometric proof under the aegis of the "dialogue." To be more precise, Plato made previous mathematics solid by introducing proof as a dialogue while simultaneously eliminating the finality of dialogue itself. In Plato's *Meno*, Socrates forces a young man who is not well educated in geometry to prove a theorem. In this demonstration, Socrates proves that there is neither "teaching" nor "learning" but only "recall." This is known as "Meno's paradox" or the paradox of pedagogy. The proof is executed in the form of a "dialogue," but a particular one in which the only thing Socrates does is to ask, "You see, Meno, that I am not teaching . . . only asking."[3] To be sure, Socrates is not teaching. The prerequisite to the dialogue is a rule that stipulates: upon acceptance of a basic premise (axiom), one must do nothing to contradict it. Proof becomes unattainable if the youth should utter anything contradictory to what he has said before. This rule is tacitly shared between Socrates and the youth.

A dialogue carried on within a common set of rules cannot be identified as a dialogue with the "other." Such a dialogue, or internal dialectic, can be converted into or considered a monologue. Socrates's method was based upon the legal institutions of Athens. Nicholas Rescher has reconsidered dialectics in terms of forms of disputation or courtroom procedure, whereby an interlocutor (prosecutor) first presents his opinion, an opponent (attorney) counterposes his point, and then the interlocutor responds to this.[4] In this way, the interlocutor's point does not have to be an absolutely apodictic, indisputable thesis. As long as no effective counterproposal is raised against the claim, it is understood to be true. In such argumentation, only the interlocutor bears the *onus probandi*, the burden of proof; the opponent is not obliged to present testimony. Socrates's method clearly follows this course. It is significant that Plato began *Meno* by describing the case of Socrates, who believed so strongly in this dialogic justice that he accepted his own death as a result of its verdict. For Socrates, even if the verdict were found to be untrue, it is the process of justice itself that is of primary importance—he acknowledged as truth only what passed through this process of justice.

In a court of law, both opponents must obey a common rule that technically allows the prosecutor and defense attorney to exchange roles at any time. Those who do not acknowledge and adhere to the legal language game are either ordered out of court or ruled incompetent by the court. In this sort of game, no matter how forcefully or enthusiastically they might oppose one another, neither opponent occupies the position of "the other." As Rescher claims, this dialogue has the potential to become a monologue. In the work of both Aristotle and Hegel, dialectics became a monologue. And though Plato's dialogues were written in the form of conversations, finally they must be considered monologues. Western philosophy thus began as an introspective—that is, monologic—*dialogue*.

What Socrates (Plato) proposed was not the idea that reason resides immanently in the world or self but the idea that only those propositions that pass through the dialogue can be acknowledged as rational. Those who reject the dialogue are considered irrational, no matter how profound or how vigorously argued their truth. It is by this measure that the pre-Socratics are "examined closely." To be rational was tantamount to taking the dialogue as a premise. Proof was compelling insofar as it was accomplished by "seeking the truth in company"[5] with others. Mathematics is a privileged mode of inquiry because its scope is greater than that of a single subjectivity. But rather than possessing this power intrinsically, mathematics's power to produce truth derives from the Platonic proposition that acknowledges as mathematics only that which has survived the dialogue of justice. After Plato, the mathematical proof came to be seen as an intersubjective cognition the scope of which extends beyond the purview of the individual.

It was dialogue understood as the source of truth that was the real object of Wittgenstein's critique. For Wittgenstein, mathematics is composed of various rule systems that cannot be reduced to any one set of rules. Furthermore, rather than limiting this account of systems to mathematics, Wittgenstein applied it to language games in general. One should not forget, however, that Wittgenstein's critique was directed primarily at the privileged discourse of mathematics and its proofs. Wittgenstein thus questioned the Platonic dialogue because it is *not* inclusive of the other, and often becomes a monologue. In order to interiorize the other, that other must share a set of common rules. But doesn't the other by definition designate only those who do not share a set of rules? Is not the dialogue only with such an other? Wittgenstein attempted in his *Philosophical Investigations* to introduce this other that could no longer be interiorized, that is, the otherness of the other. And in the course of this project he reintroduced the teaching that Plato had discarded.

The time period during which Wittgenstein worked on the *Tractatus Logico-Philosophicus* (completed in 1921) is customarily called his early period, while *Philosophical Investigations* (begun in 1937) falls within his later period. There was a long moment of silence in between. After abandoning philosophy, Wittgenstein returned to Vienna, went to the front in World War I, worked as an elementary school teacher for three years (between 1922 and 1925), and became an architect for the succeeding two years (1926–1928). It is perhaps inappropriate to view these jobs as a therapy for his neurosis—as did Wittgenstein's family and friends, who hoped he would return to philosophy. It is also wrong to regard this period as a transition between Wittgenstein's two philosophical periods, a "turn" from early to late. There is little doubt that between these two periods Wittgenstein abandoned philosophy altogether. If there is any truth to Aristotle's assertion that philosophy is high-minded because it is practiced by those who can "spare time and money," then Wittgenstein's decision to relinquish his family fortune could be understood as an abandonment of philosophy as such.

One prominent aspect of *Philosophical Investigations* is the persistent references he makes to *teaching children*. For Wittgenstein, children, like foreigners, represent the other who does not hold the same rule in common.

Someone who did not understand our language, a foreigner, who had fairly often heard someone giving the order: "Bring me a slab!," might believe that this whole series of sounds was one word corresponding perhaps to the word for "building-stone" in his language.[1]

To communicate with a foreigner or with children is to teach those who do not share a common set of rules. In this situation, the inability to share a common code is equally significant for the other; one could say that communication with the other—the one who does not share a common set of rules—invariably forms a teaching-learning relationship. Conventional theories of communication unexceptionally presuppose a shared common rule, while in dialogues with foreigners, children, and psychotics, a common rule cannot, at least initially, be assumed.

We were all at one point children and acquired language from our parents. Primary communication has always taken place in the teaching-learning relationship. Even our everyday communications entail some degree of incommensurability, resulting in the necessity of reciprocal teaching. If a common rule surfaces, it appears only as a result of this teaching-learning situation. It is this asymmetrical teaching-learning relationship that forms the fundamental precondition for communication. Indeed, what is commonly presupposed as a normal case—a dialogue *with* a common rule—is rather exceptional. Mikhail Bakhtin would call this a monologue. Wittgenstein's introduction of the other is tantamount to introducing the asymmetrical relationship.

The teaching position is not authoritarian, but is the weaker of the two because it is subordinated to someone else's acquisition of knowledge. This inferiority might be likened to the selling position in the buyer-seller relation. As Marx argued, the value that classical economists claimed to be immanent within each commodity is not in fact contained therein. If an individual commodity is not sold or exchanged, it can have neither exchange value nor use value. As we will see later, because the selling position is subordinate to the will of the buyer (to the owner of money), the selling-buying relationship, too, is asymmetrical. In classical as well as neoclassical economics this asymmetrical relationship is erased in favor of an even, smooth selling and buying process wherein selling equals buying.

C–M. First metamorphosis of the commodity, or sale. The leap taken by value from the body of the commodity into the body of the gold is the commodity's *salto mortale*, as I have called it elsewhere. If the leap falls short, it is not the commodity which is defrauded but rather its owner.[2]

In classical economics, the difference between money and commodity, or between the equivalent value form and the relative value form of the commodity, is ignored. The form of value itself is missing. For classical economics, a "common essence" (labor) is immanently embodied in every commodity, and its barometer is money. In order for such a model of economic thinking to come into existence, the *uncontrollable risk* inherent in exchange that Marx stressed must necessarily have been overlooked. With *Capital* Marx injected the static framework of classical economics with the form of value, and by so doing he managed to think from the viewpoint of the selling position.

The same asymmetry can be observed with words in the sense that they do and do not make sense. For Wittgenstein, private language did not exist. While most economists and linguists held that exchanges were organized by rules, Marx and Wittgenstein approached the phenomena of exchange in a radically different way. For Wittgenstein, "someone who did not understand our language, a foreigner" was not simply an example chosen among others, but an other who is indispensable for his "methodical doubt." For example, when one says, "Bring me a slab," there is an *internal* meaning that is understood implicitly. However, if for "the other" the word signifies something else, let's say a "building stone," one's internal meaning is called into question. This kind of internal doubt is not unlike Descartes's own radical doubt.

Wittgenstein's "other," by appearing as "a bizarre skeptic," to use Saul Kripke's term, undermines the architectonicity of our internal meaning and process. Wittgenstein says, "This was our paradox: no course of action could be determined by a rule, because every course of action can be made out to accord with the rule."[3] Kripke demonstrates this paradox in the form of mathematical equations. First, as he notes, the equation $2 + 2 = 4$ is accepted by everyone. A second equation, $2 + 3 = 6$, need not be seen as false if we understand the symbol "+" not to mean "to add" but instead "to multiply." After having encountered the second equation, we discover a common rule that satisfies conditions of both examples. Then another equation, $2 + 4 = 6$, is cited. Even in this equation, the contradiction can be resolved if a rule is fabricated such that any consequence of "+" that becomes more than 6 will be 6. In the same way, the sense or rule of the symbol "+" can be indefinitely transformed whenever a new equation is cited. The caveat is that until the new condition is encountered, the next sense or rule of "+" cannot be developed. This mechanism is applicable to language in general.

Following Kripke, let us call the "+" in the third equation *quus* instead of plus, and the equation *quaddition* instead of addition. Let us then imagine a situation in which the "other" insists that I must already have interpreted "+" as *quus* in the first equation. I cannot refute such an assertion. According to Kripke, Wittgenstein's "skeptic" appears in this very way.

It [skeptical challenge] purports to show that nothing in my mental history of past behavior—not even what an omniscient God would know—could establish whether I meant plus or quus. But then it appears to follow that there was no *fact* about me that constituted my having meant plus rather than quus. How could there be, if nothing in my internal mental history or external behavior will answer the sceptic who supposes that in fact I meant quus? If there was no such thing as my meaning plus rather than quus in the past, neither can there be any such thing in the present. When we initially presented the paradox, we perforce used language, taking present meanings for granted. Now we see, as we expected, that this provisional concession was indeed fictive. There can be no fact as to what I mean by "plus", or any other word at any time. The ladder must finally be kicked away.[4]

Doubt of this sort is achieved only by developing the teaching position to its full extent. (I cannot agree with Kripke, however, when he concludes this paradox with the "precedence of community"; as we will see later, this conclusion is inaccurate and misleading.) The important point he makes is that the undecidability that arises from a confrontation with the other is "not even what an omniscient God would know." The other is not replaceable with *God*, because an omniscient God is not the other, but merely an idealization of the self.

What draws a clear distinction between Cartesian doubt and Wittgensteinian doubt, then, is not simply their different attitudes toward the evidence of self—that Descartes came to obtain evidence of the doubting self beginning with his own doubt, while Wittgenstein was led to deny the evidence of self by his doubt. Instead, what is more relevant is that Descartes began with the suspicion that God might be deceiving him and ended up securing or grounding the *cogito* by God. Descartes thus attempted to guarantee evidence of the self by means of the other as God. It is clear that there is a "fatal leap" hidden in Descartes's method, though Cartesianism emerged as a suppression of this leap. On the other hand, Wittgenstein never represents the other who undermines the internal certainty as God—the *absolute* other. The Wittgensteinian other is always a child and a foreigner—the *relative* other.

This approach shows a striking contrast to the following statement from the *Tractatus*: "Whereof one cannot speak, thereof one must be silent."[5] In this case, "Whereof one cannot speak" refers to God. In *Philosophical Investigations* Wittgenstein no longer follows this approach. Allan Janik and Stephen Toulmin have observed that Wittgenstein, unlike Russell, retained the Kantian problematic, and that what Russell offered Wittgenstein was merely a new technique. They write, "If this diagnosis is once accepted, no difficulty remains in reconciling the 'logical' and the 'ethical' aspects of Wittgenstein's ideas. The *point* of his book—as he himself was in due course to insist—is an *ethical* one; its formal techniques alone are drawn from propositional logic."[6] But in *Philosophical Investigations*, Wittgenstein no longer sustained the Kantian distinction between science/logic and ethics/beauty. Of course this is not to suggest that he had become indifferent to ethics. Instead, he discovered an ethical problem within language in and of itself. The following statement by Kripke might shed light on how Wittgenstein shared a kind of Kierkegaardian ethical concern.

There can be no such thing as meaning anything by any word. Each new application we make is a leap in the dark; any present intention could be interpreted so as to accord with anything we may choose to do. So there can be neither accord, nor conflict.[7]

It is noteworthy that, even in the face of such a formidable situation, Wittgenstein never resorted to the appeal to God. What should be underscored here is that it is Wittgenstein's "secularness" that prompted him to meditate upon philosophical problems from the standpoint of teaching. Indeed, this "leap in the dark" accords with what Marx called the commodity's "fatal leap," and it is perhaps only Marx who shared the interest in approaching the problem from the standpoint of selling. Herein lies their *Ethica*.

A commodity appears at first sight an extremely obvious, trivial thing. But its analysis brings out that it is a very strange thing, abounding in metaphysical subtleties and theological niceties.[8]

It is possible to observe the commodity's "fatal leap" in Søren Kierkegaard's *Sickness unto Death*. What Kierkegaard called the ultimate form of despair (sickness unto death) was a state of the self: though the self has to be founded by the other, "it despairs of wanting in despair to be oneself." Is this not reminiscent of the unsold commodity? Indeed, it is in this way that the commodity itself can be understood to contain a "theological" problem. But classical economists and Hegelians had little or no interest in the crisis of exchange, for both observed the value of the commodity ex post facto and from the perspective of a preestablished harmony. Seen in this light, Marx's critique of Hegel in *Capital* is not a mere overturning of Hegelian dialectics, but is more like the establishment of a kind of Kierkegaardian "qualitative dialectic." Classical economists maintained that the commodity emerged as a consolidation of exchange value and use value. In Marx, however, this synthesis appears closer to the Kierkegaardian view of the human as a synthesis of finite and infinite, because for a commodity to be a synthesis of use value and exchange value, a "leap" must be made as a rite of passage. Both classical economics and Hegel interpreted this phenomenon from the wrong direction, beginning from the *result* and not with the conditions of the exchange.

It is important to note that both Marx and Wittgenstein, unlike Descartes and Kierkegaard, dealt with the problem of exchange secularly. This peculiarity, however, does not derive from the Marxian base/superstructure formula, in which the economy forms the base while the superstructure, though relatively autonomous, is defined by the base. Rather, the economy should be understood as an autonomous superstructure, so that any analysis of the commodity requires one to look beyond metaphysical and theological problems. It is futile to look for Marx's philosophy anywhere but in *Capital*; paradoxically, it is also futile to include Marx's discourses on the commodity under the rubric "philosophy." Selling and teaching are not useful for explaining philosophical issues in plain language, but they are the kinds of things that, though confronted on a daily basis by philosophers, are rarely scrutinized by them. It is in selling and teaching that the asymmetrical communicative relationship with the other is laid bare. Philosophical discourses have maintained their ground by erasing this asymmetry.

The asymmetrical relationship with the other that I have been describing will now be examined in the context of "Wittgenstein's architecture." After Paul Engelmann designed the Kundmanngasse house at the request of Wittgenstein's sister, Margaret Stonborough Wittgenstein, it was completed, with Wittgenstein's participation, in two years. Wittgenstein's legendary obsessive perfectionism made it impossible for the house to be off the mark by even one millimeter. He called the house "my architecture." Although to a certain extent this precisionism is reminiscent of the methodical spirit that animates the *Tractatus*, there are clear differences. The design was Engelmann's, and he remained devoted throughout the process. Furthermore, Wittgenstein's sister, who was intensely individualistic, insisted that the house reflect her own lifestyle. In a strict sense, the house is not really "Wittgenstein's architecture."

But it was not to insist upon his authorship that Wittgenstein called it "my architecture." He did not think of architecture as a simple realization of an author's design; had this been the case, he could have rejected Engelmann's design. From the beginning, the building was determined by various external factors such as his sister's taste, the family circle (including maids and houseboys), the relation to the surrounding buildings, and so on. Wittgenstein's precisionism by no means indicates his total domination. He thus did not try to create every single element from scratch: more than anyone, Wittgenstein understood that this building, and architecture in general, was the result of a dialogue between the various participants.

Perhaps nothing is more irrelevant to architecture than the notion that it is the realization of a design *qua idea*. Far more dominant factors are the dialogue with and persuasion of the client and the collaboration with other staff members. The design as initially conceived is destined to be transformed during the course of its execution. As with Wittgenstein, it is similar to a game "where we play and—make up rules as we go along."

Doesn't the analogy between language and games throw light here? We can easily imagine people amusing themselves in a field by playing with a ball so as to start various existing games, but playing many without finishing them and in between throwing the ball aimlessly into the air, chasing one another with the ball and bombarding one another for a joke and so on. And now someone says: The whole time they are playing a ball-game and following definite rules at every throw.

And is there not also the case where we play and—make up the rules as we go along? And there is even one where we alter them—as we go along.[1]

No architect can predict the results of construction. No architecture exists out of context. Architecture is an event par excellence. As Wittgenstein maintained, it is the same with mathematics. Plato admired the architect as a metaphor, but despised the architect as a man because the actual architect and architecture are fully exposed to contingency. However, this state of architectural contingency does not imply that the actual architecture, as opposed to some putative ideal architecture, is secondary and in danger of collapse. Rather it implies that no architect can determine a design free from the relationship with the other (the client). All architects face the unknowable other. Architecture, in other words, is a form of communication, and this communication is conditioned to take place without common rules because it takes place with the other, who does not follow a commensurable set of rules.

The architect can be exempted from the contingency generated in the encounter with this relative other only if backed up by an absolute power. Some architects no doubt dream of this impossible situation. Though architecture is an event, and thereby necessarily contingent, we need not invoke the poet to refute Plato's use of the architect as a metaphor; to do so would only lead us to another sanctification. Instead, if one wants to discard architecture as metaphor, one can simply substitute secular architecture as a metaphor.

When Wittgenstein raised an objection to the formalistic/architectonic project in mathematics, he stressed the determinism inherent in mathematics. In the Egypt of Plato's time, the calculation of the "ratio of the circumference of the circle to the diameter" had already been devised out of practical necessity; for Plato, however, this could not be acknowledged as mathematics, which had to be solid and deduced from axioms. But why isn't the calculation of the "ratio of the circumference of the circle to the diameter" mathematics? If only those principles deduced from axioms were allowed to be called mathematics, it would have been impossible for mathematics to develop in the first place. Moreover, it would never be possible to explain the fact that formal mathematics is applicable to the natural world. It is hard to imagine that non-Euclidean geometricians, who allegedly occasioned a crisis in mathematics, managed to construct an alternative geometry merely by transforming Euclid's fifth postulate. If this had occurred, Einstein's ability to apply non-Euclidean geometry in the development of his theory of relativity could not be explained. Theories of mathematical foundations are enabled by a disregard of the naive but basic question, why is mathematics applicable?

The non-Euclidean geometricians of the late nineteenth century originally had strong astronomical interests and intended to proceed along their non-Euclidean vectors even to the point of omitting axiomatic foundations as such. But because mathematics has always been, in a sense, applied mathematics, it has sustained its applicability. This *mystery* of applicability formed an aporia for those who attempted to preserve mathematical foundations, and in due time it paved the way for Gödel's proof. But Gödel's proof did not make mathematics impossible, as commonly believed. Since his proof paralyzed and rendered problematic only those systems that were deducible from axioms, it liberated mathematics in general from the unfair burden of solidity imposed on it by outsiders.

Until the eighteenth century, mathematicians regarded mathematics as a kind of game. This too contradicts the serious, axiomatic solidity of mathematics. Thus the development of mathematics has continued unaffected by solidity. When Wittgenstein rejected the sine qua non of the formal system—that it must be solidly deduced from axioms—he introduced the other who does not share a common set of rules, a gesture tantamount to introducing *other sets of rules* that cannot be interiorized within one and the same rule. Gödel demonstrated his proof after translating the foundations of non-Euclidean geometry into those of Euclidean geometry and then into natural numbers. Wittgenstein relates this procedure:

What is it to coordinate one system of proofs with another? It involves a translation rule by means of which proved propositions of the one can be translated into proved propositions of the other.

Now it is possible to imagine some—or all—of the proof systems of present-day mathematics as having been coordinated in such a way with one system, say that of Russell. So that all proofs could be carried out in the system, even though in a roundabout way. So would there then be only the single system—no longer that many?—But then it must surely be possible to show of the *one* system that it can be resolved into the many.—*One* part of the system will process the properties of trigonometry, another those of algebra, and so on. Thus one can say that different techniques are used in these parts.[2]

Wittgenstein objected to the attempts of Russell and others to ground all mathematical practices in set theory. According to Russell's idea, 1, 2, 3, . . . can be translated into 1, 1+1, (1+1) + 1, ... However, something like 84 × 23 would be too cumbersome if described in this Russellian manner. As Wittgenstein's notes, "A mathematical proof must be perspicuous."[3] Only with the emergence of the decimal system could the calculation become so.

Russell believed that to calculate using 1, 1+1, (1+1) +1, . . . would give mathematics a foundation, and was therefore essential, whereas for Wittgenstein even a calculation that made use of the decimal system was a "mathematical invention" and a system of proofs in and of itself. "I want to say: if you have a proof-pattern that cannot be taken in, and by a change in notation you turn it into one that can, then you are producing a proof, where there was none before."[4] For Wittgenstein, it was no longer necessary to prove mathematical systems by means of a "general foundation." As he wrote, "It is not something behind the proof, but the proof, that proves."[5] New forms of expression or new mathematical proofs automatically produce new concepts by themselves.

Now surely one could simply say: if a man had invented calculating in the decimal system—that would have been a mathematical invention!—Even if he had already got Russell's *Principia Mathematica*.[6]

It [mathematics] forms ever new rules: is always building new roads for traffic; by extending the network of the old ones.[7]

But the mathematician is not a discoverer: he is an inventor.[8]

From time to time it happens in mathematics that identical theorems arise from different fields and contexts. Rather than considering them as one and the same, Wittgenstein, who understood mathematics as consisting of multiple systems, considered that they belong to different systems of rules. He wrote, "I should like to say: mathematics is a MOTLEY of techniques of proof.—And upon this is based its manifold applicability and its importance."[9] Thus what Wittgenstein objected to was founding multiple systems of rules upon a single system. Mathematical polysystems, however, are not completely separate and unrelated. Though they are translatable to (exchangeable with) each other, they do not share the same system. He gave the name "family resemblances" to such "a complicated network of similarities overlapping and crisscrossing."[10]

Instead of producing something common to all that we call language, I am saying that these phenomena have no one thing in common which makes us use the same word for all,—but that they are related to one another in many different ways. And it is because of this relationship, or these relationships, that we call them all "language."[11]

Likewise, the phenomena grouped together under the term mathematics are polysystems that cannot be centralized. Wittgenstein stressed this heterogeneity not only because mathematics deals with heterogeneous nature in a practical manner—no less than various sciences do—but also because heterogeneity came from an acknowledgment of the other who cannot be interiorized. Wittgenstein's critique of formalism, then, was focused on its tendency to exclude the otherness of the other, that is, the contingency of the relation to the other. This contingency—that even an omniscient God could not take in—can never be formalized.

Wittgenstein, like Kripke, insisted on the priority of social language to private language. But this bald assertion of the superiority of social language to private language (and solipsism) should be accepted provisionally. Though Wittgenstein disavowed solipsism, his real objection was to the solipsism inherent in intersubjectivity, wherein a mathematical proof is formed. It should be noted that solipsism not only acknowledges and in fact privileges the existence of the self, but it also asserts that what is true of the self must be universal- ly true: in order for the latter to be possible, the other must already have been interior- ized to the self. I would also like to define the term *dialogue*: It designates only the dialogic confrontation with the other who does not share a common set of rules. In other words, a true dialogue is asymmetrical. If the distinction between symmetrical and asymmetrical dialogue is not maintained, discussions concerning dialogue that take place within the frameworks of different "language games" might be seen as identical. In fact, a similar confusion has occurred.

Wittgenstein's concept of "language game," for example, has often been identified with Saussure's *langue*. In fact, like Saussure, Wittgenstein employs the game of chess as an explanatory metaphor or figure. Chess is important because it offers an example of the formal aspect of language. In the chess game the rules of the game are determined in the differential system of relations between chessmen. Chess would become a completely different game if the functions and arrangements of the chessmen were altered. The chess metaphor shows that language is a differential formal system independent of its references, and that, conversely, the latter are products of the system itself. Wittgenstein's theory of the language game, by contrast, was proposed in order to deny this formalist premise.

Moreover, not only the figure of chess but metaphors of games in general tend to lead us to the conventional preconception that a rule must be able to be explicitly given. Grammar, for example, is usually understood as a rule of language. But does one who speaks Japanese know its grammar? Having originally been invented as a method to learn foreign and classical languages, grammar is less a rule than a regulation that, if not mastered, makes language acquisition very difficult for foreigners. The grammar of one's native language, in contrast, is not only unnecessary but also impossible to conceive. Consider the fact that before the advent of modern nationalism, people did not even dream that there could be grammars of their vernacular languages.

The rules of languages are constructed not from the standpoint of those who already speak them, but from the standpoint of "foreigners" who wish to learn them. I myself do not need to, and cannot, learn the grammar of the Japanese that I speak. Yet, when a foreigner speaks Japanese, I can point out his grammatical mistakes. I know Japanese grammar despite my inability to prove the grammatical basis for the foreigner's mistakes. All I can say is, "we just don't say it that way," implying that I "do not know" the Japanese grammar, I only know the uses of Japanese.

Parents do not teach their children the rules of language, they simply talk to them and correct their mistakes when each child begins to speak. The parents do not know the rules of language, they simply practice them. "When I obey a rule, I do not choose. I obey the rule *blindly*."[1]

We can teach a child the grammar of a language only if that child already knows the language. As demonstrated by Plato, "Meno's paradox" could be read in this way: "I have just said that you are a rascal, and now you ask me if I can teach you, when I say there is no such thing as teaching, only recollection."[2] This shows the impossibility of presenting a rule explicitly, even if there is one.

Nevertheless, teaching does exist. In the case of Meno's paradox, the boy who proved a geometric theorem through the conversation with Socrates had "already" been taught a rule. And yet, as Plato claimed, because the teacher can never present the rule explicitly, there is no such thing as "teaching." Within the teaching-learning of rules, there occurs a *leap* that cannot be explained *rationally*. Plato attempted to solve this paradox by the doctrine of *anamnesis*, or recollection. This doctrine assumes that there is something essential and identical within everybody. In the history of modern philosophy, this doctrine has taken many forms, including the a priori form, the transcendental ego, and transformational grammar. All of these are mere metamorphoses of the myth of *anamnesis*; each fabricated as a result of the ex post facto presupposition that emerges from the teaching-learning situation or event.

Wittgenstein, by contrast, considered this relation or event as a natural historical fact that did not require further explanation.

It is sometimes said that animals do not talk because they lack the mental capacity. And this means: "they do not think, and that is why they do not talk." But—they simply do not talk. Or to put it better: they do not use language—if we except the most primitive forms of language.—Commanding, questioning, recounting, chatting, are as much a part of our natural history as walking, eating, drinking, playing.[3]

This means that we talk not because we know the rules, but simply because we do. This is a "natural historical fact" that cannot and need not be justified or grounded. For example, we learn how to count not because we have mastered the rules, but because, "Calculating is a phenomenon which we know from calculating. As language is a phenomenon which we know from our language."[4]

In the preceding passage, Wittgenstein is not saying that animals do participate in a language game in the broad sense; instead, he means that they are "the other." In ancient societies, foreigners' speech was often likened to animal talk, and, conversely, animals were revered as the other. All the accounts that Wittgenstein employed refer to the other who does not share a common rule.

What is crucial, as I have already implied, is that another language must necessarily be invoked in order to understand a rule of language. If we assume that a rule can be presented explicitly, we assume that the foreigner has already been interiorized. Indeed, we believe that we can stand in the foreigner's stead anytime we wish. Used in this way, "foreigner" does not designate the other; it makes no difference if a compatriot appears in his place. Thus the notion that a rule can be explicitly presented—no matter how it is used—results only in a monologue, which is to say in a dialogue with the interiorized other.

We understand a person to be accepted by the community as long as she or he "obeys the rule"; by following the rules of English, the person will be understood by the English-speaking community. As Kripke noted, Wittgenstein reversed this proposition: the person will be understood as being "not obedient to the rule" if he or she is not accepted by the community. This slight transformation is radical, but it is not easily understood. Even Kripke, who stressed the importance of this shift, finally insisted on the precedence of community.

This situation can better be described as follows: whether or not I know the meaning of a word hinges on whether or not my use of the word is accepted by the other understood as community. If I am wrong, the other will laugh or say, "it is wrong." And since no rule can be presented as such, the community can simply say "no." That it is impossible to "obey a rule" *privately* is the same as it being impossible to present the rule explicitly. Wittgenstein's well-known definition, "the meaning of a word is its use in the language," should be understood neither as a denial of meaning nor as an insistence on meaning as pragmatics. Instead, it suggests that we know the use or rule of language practically but not theoretically. "And hence also 'obeying a rule' is a practice. And to *think* one is obeying a rule is not to obey a rule. Hence it is not possible to obey a rule 'privately': otherwise thinking one was obeying a rule would be the same thing as obeying it."[5] Even if I believe that I know the rules of a foreign language, I cannot prove that I really know them practically unless the other acknowledges it. And, though I speak Japanese according to its rules, I do not know the rules explicitly; I obey the rules unconsciously. What Wittgenstein so obstinately attempted to do, then, was to assert the asymmetry inherent in the relationship with the other and, at the same time, to offer a critique of the kind of thinking that ignores asymmetry.

Saussure's work has caused us to believe that we are able to know the rules of a language. Unlike linguists who had taken language as an objective field, he began with the "speaking subject." Saussure's idea of *langue*, then, is not to be understood as an institution like a national language, but instead as a form that makes the national language possible. But taking a subject as a point of departure leaves us with no possible way to access this *langue* that simultaneously regulates the other and produces or composes the subject itself.

When Saussure suggests that language itself can be nothing but a relational system of pure values without positive terms, he is unwittingly comparing and translating one language to another. The same can be said of Plato's *idea*, which is a general concept unaffected by the differences between languages. In the case of Saussure, however, he was aware that in the comparison or translation of two languages, the translator, even if bilingual, necessarily places himself or herself within one or the other of these languages at a time. There is no universal, neutral position in between languages. This asymmetry can never be made symmetrical. However, as did other structuralists, Saussure omitted asymmetry from the other aspects of his research. To return to a previous point, solipsism is an omission of asymmetry that identifies the I as the we.

It was by this process that structural linguistics became subsumed into phenomenological solipsism. This explains why Derrida found it necessary to initiate his critique of structuralism by way of a deconstruction of Husserl. Derrida asserts that what is regarded as self-evident in phenomenology is dependent on the "present-to-itself," on "hearing-oneself-speak." The "voice *is* consciousness,"[6] which is to say that consciousness is essentially a dialogue with oneself—a monologue. Saussure's "subject of speech" is not unlike the phenomenological subject who "hears oneself speak"; it is already a monologue in which the subject who hears the speech—*the other*—is interiorized within the subject who speaks.

Derrida locates a gap in this identity or subject created as a result of "speaking/hearing"; or perhaps it is more accurate to say that he identifies this gap as the enabling structure for subjectivity—Derrida calls this structure *trace* or *la différance*. "Such a trace is—if we can employ this language without immediately contradicting it or crossing it out as we proceed—more 'primordial' than what is phenomenologically primordial."[7] Rather than rejecting phonocentrism/logocentrism out of hand, Derrida reveals them to be dependent on the concealment of *différance*. Derrida's location of this structure, his deconstruction, resembles Gödel's strategy that "attacks Russell from within"; that is why Derrida's critique always takes the form of a proof. Though Derrida attempts to avoid a direct confrontation with the metaphysical apparatus of philosophical discourses, this proof has formed the basis of metaphysics since Plato.

Wittgenstein attempted to dismantle this proof from without by introducing the other, something accomplishable only from the teaching position, from the topos where a common language game (community) can no longer function as a premise. It is only in such a topos that we confront the other. It should be understood, then, that the other is not subsumed within the internal monologue, the Hegelian "another self-consciousness," nor the stranger/monster that cultural anthropologists refer to. By the other I mean the one who is essentially indifferent to *me*.

Author's Note 1

Bakhtin held that Saussure's model of linguistics was subjectivist—"an individualization of the general language." Bakhtin stressed that we should instead begin with the "language spoken to the other." However, it is not quite enough to emphasize this aspect of "being told to the other." To this must be added the other *who follows the incommensurable set of rules;* it is at that point that the teaching position will be achieved. Bakhtin's objective linguistics situates itself so that it can see both speaker and listener from above. Accordingly, concepts of "dialogue" and "polyphony" tend to be understood as a transcendental position. However, Bakhtin used Dostoyevsky's monologic *Notes from the Underground* as an example of a polyphonic work because the protagonist "talks to the other" who can never be interiorized within himself. Though the protagonist tries to include the other inside the space of his language game, he fails because, unlike Hegel's "another self-consciousness," the other is indifferent to him. Bakhtin saw communication less from the aspect of simply talking to the other, and more from teaching the other. Like Saussure, Bakhtin believed that language is social. But, as we will see in the next chapter, for Bakhtin society should be clearly distinguished from community: the language spoken to the other will become social, dialogic, and polyphonic only if the other is an outsider to the community where a common set of rules is shared; the dialogue within a "community" is merely a monologue. If it is read in this way, Bakhtin's "polyphonic" begins to correspond to Wittgenstein's "MOTLEY."

Author's Note 2

Hayek attacks socialism as something contradictory to liberalism. At the same time, however, he uses the word "society" to refer to "spontaneous order."

The family, the farm, the plant, the firm, the corporation and the various associations, and all the public institutions including government, are organizations which in turn are integrated into a more comprehensive spontaneous order. It is advisable to reserve the term "society" for this spontaneous overall order so that we may distinguish it from all the organized smaller groups which will exist within it, as well as from such smaller and more or less isolated groups as the horde, the tribe, or the clan, whose members will at least in some respects act under a central direction for common purposes.[8]

In Marx, too, "society" is consistently grasped less as a community or system than as communication between a multitude of communities and systems. As a result, society is linked to *Naturwüchsigkeit*.

Despite the fact that Hayek attempts to make Marx out to be a statist or an archist, as many Marxists have done, his position is, ironically, very similar to Marx's. Their difference is explicitly manifest in the difference between spontaneous order and *Naturwüchsigkeit*: while Hayek's notion of spontaneous order is protected, as it were, by the "invisible hand [of God]," for Marx, "society" always contains a critical leap inherent in communication/exchange.

We have examined how Wittgenstein singled out
children and foreigners as the other who does not
follow a common set of rules. In so doing he discovered a kind of exchange between communities unlike that governed by communication
executed under a single set of rules and within one community. Marx underscores this
in *Capital*:

The exchange of commodities begins where
communities have their boundaries, at
their points of contact with other communities, or with members of the latter. However, as soon as products
have become commodities in the
external relations of a community, they also, by reaction,
become commodities in the
internal life of the community.[1]

As I have already remarked, the
exchange of products springs up at the
points where different families, tribes or
communities come into contact; for at the
dawn of civilization it is not private individuals but families, tribes, etc. that meet on an
independent footing. Different communities
find different means of production and different
means of subsistence in their natural environment.
Hence their modes of production and living, as well as
their products, are different. It is this spontaneously
developed difference which, when different communities
come into contact, calls forth the mutual exchange of products and the consequent gradual conversion of those products
into commodities.[2]

These descriptions are different in quality from the logical description with which he analyzed the form of value, because here the occurrences of exchange and money are speculated upon from a historical (genetic) perspective. Not surprisingly, there have been debates among Marxists about this descriptive difference. Though his logical description of the emergence of money is ahistorical, what Marx describes in the above passages is not limited to the early stage of culture, either. Even at present, exchanges occur between communities that do not share a common set of rules. Thus, community should be redefined primarily as a space enclosed within a certain system of rules, irrespective of its actual scale. Village, race, nation-state, Western Hemisphere, and even the self (as a self-contained monologic space) may be seen as communities.

Marx used the term "social" to describe the peculiar characteristics of exchange between communities that do not share a common set of rules, as distinct from the exchange that takes place within a community.

The mysterious character of the commodity-form consists therefore simply in the fact that the commodity reflects the social characteristics of men's own labor as objective characteristics of the products of labor themselves, as the socio-natural properties of these things. Hence it also reflects the social relation of the producers to the sum total of labour as a social relation between objects, a relation which exists apart from and outside the producers.

As the foregoing analysis has already demonstrated, this fetishism of the world of commodities arises from the peculiar social character of the labor which produces them.[3]

This "social character of the labor" must be "peculiar to the labor which produces *commodities*," because the labor within a community cannot attain such a "social character" by itself; this is less a general characteristic of labor than something that is attributed to labor by the exchange of commodities. Therefore, this "social character" must be singled out not from labor per se, but from the exchange that takes place "in between" communities.

A commodity is exchanged with money, with which other commodities are in turn purchased. All commodities, then, must exist in a form that can be made equivalent (according to a certain ratio). Why? For classical economics it is because a common essence, human labor, is contained within each commodity. However, the contrary is actually the case. Because certain commodities have been physically exchanged, they may be understood to have a common essence. Suppose I purchase an orange with the royalty I have earned from this book. According to classical economics, my intellectual labor and the manual labor of a worker from Florida, or somewhere else, are equivalent. These two activities are seen as common human labor because they have been deemed equivalent, and not vice versa—they are not equivalent because they are seen as common human labor. Though we are not always aware of it, we are connected to others all over the world through the mechanisms of selling and buying. The "social" depends on a certain, inevitable impossibility of knowledge (an unconsciousness of the social relation). Marx almost always used the term "social" in this very sense.

Men do not therefore bring the products of their labor into relation with each other as values because they see these objects merely as the material integuments of homogeneous human labor. The reverse is true: by equating their different products to each other in exchange as values, they equate their different kinds of labor as human labor. They do this without being aware of it. Value, therefore, does not have its description branded on its forehead; it rather transforms every product of labor into a social hieroglyphic. Later on, men try to decipher the hiero-glyphic, to get behind the secret of their own social product: for the characteristic which objects of utility have of being values is as much men's social product as is their language. The belated sci-entific discovery that the products of labor, insofar as they are values, are merely the material expressions of the human labor expended to produce them, marks an epoch in the history of mankind's development, but by no means banishes the semblance of objectivity possessed by the social characteristics of labor.[4]

Social exchanges, in which rules—albeit constituted ex post facto—are destined to be altered, are like Wittgen-stein's game "where we play and—make up rules as we go along." They require a "leap." "Social" exchange/ communication, to cite Marx's term from *The German Ideology*, is the intercourse (*Verkehr*) that forms a hetero-geneous system whose totality cannot be grasped. Therefore, society must be unequivocally distinguished from community. And such a social space in between communities—though an invisible entity—is called the marketplace. I would like to call this the "intercrossing space." When this in-between space expands to subsume all the individual communities to form one single gigan-tic community, a certain regularity (system of rules) appears wherein economics would become possible as a "science." Classical economics, which departs from the model of an enclosed unitary equilibrate system and instead views economical phenomena from a physical model, appeared in exactly in this way.

That exchanges occur between different systems of rules becomes the basis for money's continuous conver-sion into capital. This occurs because capital, as self-increasing money, discovers its surplus value in the difference between systems. This is also why capitalism is dependent on internal crisis. Ultimately, the danger (and the contradiction) inherent in selling cannot be resolved. Both classical and neoclassical schools, and even Marxists, are trapped in the model of an equilibrate system. The equilibrate effect of a market economy as such can be grasped only ex post facto in the process of individual exchange, that is, in the discontinuity between the merciless selection of the owner of money and the fatal leap of the owner of the commodity. Engels did not recognize the correlation between the "social and anarchic factors" of the market economy; he believed that simply by rationally controlling the anarchic factor, socialism would emerge. Engels believed that society should be converted into a community/unitary system, a belief that is simply an extension of classical economists.

Lévi-Strauss criticized this concept of exchange as a bias of modern capitalism. For Lévi-Strauss kinship systems are already full-blown exchange systems, where the gift and the return automatically play the role of exchanging products. It must be noted, however, that an uncivilized society is not the same as a primitive society; so-called uncivilized societies are communities that, at certain historical stages of development, have closed themselves to intercourse with other societies. This can occur at any historical stage. What is taboo in such communities, however, is not incest, as Lévi-Strauss claimed, but the threat of an exteriority (otherness) that would threaten their self-sufficient system. Therefore, to regard such an exchange within a community as *exchange*—seeing exchange in terms of the "general economics" of Georges Bataille—results in the omission of the enigma of social exchange in and of itself. Although this would appear to deny prevalent theories of modern economics, it in fact conforms to the most modern way of thinking (the most neoclassical-like school), which is illustrated in the discovery of the cybernetic equilibrate system in uncivilized societies. The very thoughts that appear to deny self or solipsism themselves conform to solipsism.

It is a fallacy to believe that solipsism may be breached by privileging language over consciousness as does Richard Rorty. Rorty's "linguistic turn" is itself simply another form of solipsism. Descartes is commonly criticized for his attempt to found the certainty of knowledge upon the evidence of the autonomous subject or self. But it was not Descartes who initiated introspective philosophical meditation—almost every philosopher since Socrates engaged in this mode of thought. On the contrary, the importance of the Cartesian *cogito* is that it emerged as a way to destroy the monologue: "What is true of the self must be true universally."

Eighteen **The Linguistic Turn and *Cogito***

Descartes turned to consciousness as a means of securing certainty because philosophy had until that time been dependent upon language, especially grammar. (It was the communality of the European languages that formed the foundation of this philosophy.) Stability was insured by following the conventions and common rules of the community. *Cogito ergo sum* is a kind of Being in the topos "in between" (as difference between) communities. Descartes's *Discourse on Method* was written from the standpoint of the "anthropologist" as described by Lévi-Strauss, though Lévi-Strauss himself harshly criticized Descartes. Rather than starting from the certainty of the internal process, as commonly believed,

Descartes asserted that certainty was merely a dream fostered within this European community. He therefore attempted to ground his method on something more substantial than this dream.

Descartes observed that the proof offered by the *cogito* was sufficient only for him, and not for others. Moreover, he refused to accept dialogue as a guarantor of certainty. While in conventional introspective thought the self is understood as a particular case of the general self, the Cartesian *cogito* proved to be a discovery of a *singular self*, totally disconnected from the circuit of particular-general selves. In this confrontation with singularity, Descartes had no choice but to resort to God as guarantor of certainty. The attempt to prove the existence of God by starting from the *cogito*, however, is itself a *para doxa*—nothing more than circular reasoning. It is what Kierkegaard would call a "leap" (qualitative dialectics). In place of the particularity-generality circuit Descartes introduced singularity-universality.

This aspect of Cartesianism was ignored by successive philosophers. Immanuel Kant considered the *cogito* an a priori and empty form that could be universally applied; individual subjectivity was for Kant a *particular* kind of *general* transcendental subjectivity. Hegel called "this same" subjectivity *Geist*, and Husserl, by identifying his own transcendental phenomenological "neo-Cartesianism," attempted to carry Cartesianism even further. Instead of presupposing this universal subject in the way Kant had, Husserl attempted to return to a singular *cogito*—he called this methodical solipsism. Starting from such a position, he derived the other (other-self) and then inter-subjectivity (objectivity). However, this other self is not "the other"; it is instead a "metamorphosis of the self" into a "self-involvement-into the *self*" and thus devoid of otherness. The "other" is also absent in Heidegger, who criticized Husserlian phenomenology in order to shift emphasis from the subject of thinking to "Being." Heidegger attempted to resolve the problem of the Husserlian other by introducing the *Mitsein* (Being-with), but this only resulted in the ultimate community based on the exclusion of the other: Nazism. This all invariably returned to the circuit of particularity-generality, because in the circuit of singularity-universality a certain "leap" is inevitably confronted.

Perhaps it was this circuit that Wittgenstein, too, attempted to short-circuit. Wittgenstein's architecture should be considered in this light. "Wittgenstein's architecture" can be so called not because it is an expression of the author Wittgenstein, but because this house is a singular event that occurs around the name Wittgenstein. Kripke objected to Russell's idea of reducing the proper name to a set of descriptions.[1] It is not the point of this book, however, to discuss this specific problem in detail, though it can be stressed that Wittgenstein was neither a descriptivist like Russell nor an anti-descriptivist like Kripke.

Descriptivists would reduce the "individual" to a bundle of its predicates or sets. This is a reduction that takes place within the circuit of particularity-generality. Structuralism, too, operates within this circuit: it reduces the text to a bundle of transformational rules. Yet the question remains, Why do we continue to identify a certain text by its author's name? It is not because of our resistant romanticist notion of "authorship." If something that is irreducible to structure continues to exist, we seem to have no choice but to affix a proper name to the text. Descriptivism dominates because it works in tandem with a scientific ideology that sees individuals in either general or regular terms. Though in the general sense of the term, history written with proper names is mere narrative, in reality history without proper names cannot even be a history. In a precise sense, even natural science belongs to natural history—*this* natural history, a history that could have existed in other ways, but has existed in this very way. In this way this universe, this galactic system, and this earth are all proper names. On the other hand, Kripke, who debated Russell's position from the viewpoint of "possible worlds," maintained that "primal baptism" in the community precedes the proper name.

Again, this idea cannot distinguish between community and society. Linguists, for example, exclude proper names from their objects of analysis not only because proper names reinforce the illusion of the direct link between words and things, but also because proper names, being untranslatable into any other language, cannot be interiorized by any of the systems of *langue*. Does not this externality of proper names that resists being interiorized within any *langue* or community indicate that the names are themselves "social"? Proper names involve an otherness or contingency that can never be interiorized by a self or a community. This can be understood simply by examining the communicative relation between Kripke's giver and receiver of the name; the relationship is that of teaching-learning, where a common rule has not yet been established. Therefore, it is with the proper name, which linguists ignore, that the sociality in communication is fully exposed.

The singularity of an individual is manifest in a proper name because a singularity—as distinct from particularity—cannot be reduced to any bundle of sets, to any generality. Singularity, contrary to the nuances it may convey, has nothing to do with bourgeois individualism; paradoxically enough, singularity is inseparable from society, from being "in between" communities—it is the space where Descartes initiated his method of radical doubt, a space that was eventually absorbed and enclosed within the paradigm of community. It is therefore futile to deny the Cartesianism that was constituted around such a problematic merely from the orientation of language.

Critics of Descartes commonly invoke as part of their critique either language or dialogue. Some critics might suggest that there exists only the optional form (signifier), which then produces the bifurcation of subject/object or internal sense/referent. As we have seen already, this kind of critique does not derive from linguistics or psychoanalysis but from formalism in the most general sense.[2]

Another criticism of Descartes stresses the importance of dialogue. Rescher, criticizing "the egocentric perspective of modern epistemology since Descartes," writes: "The skeptic in effect emerges as unwilling to abide by the evidential ground rules that govern the management of rational deliberation along the established lines."[3] Stressing this point, Rescher continues: "To abandon these in favor of some putatively personalized standards of inquiry—withdrawing to the use of private criteria, however well intentioned—is to secede from the community of rational reasoners and to abandon the project of rationality as such."[4] The key terms, such as Rescher's "dialogue" and Jürgen Habermas's "communicative rationality," however, cannot be equated with the dialogue in the social field as long as they are set within a community where a common rule is shared. Rather, they function as exclusionary to the non-Western "other." But Wittgenstein's criticism of private language should not be read in these terms; neither should it be read as postmodern pluralism, as it is in the work of Jean-François Lyotard.

The essence of Cartesian doubt can be found in its refusal to be reduced to either universalism or relativism. No matter how critical we are of Descartes, we find ourselves, though in different contexts, occupying the same position that he did with regard to this problem. Indeed, our criticisms of him are variants of his own position. For example, his "grammar" and "custom" can be interchanged with "paradigm" and "episteme." The debate in the philosophy of science between relativists and universalists over the problem of the incommensurability of different paradigms is a variant of the same problem already taken up by Descartes. Just as Descartes's "proof" failed, this debate will never reach a solution. Practical sciences do not suffer in the least if there is no solution in the philosophy of science.

For the moment, let us return to Descartes's proof of the existence of God: I doubt because I am imperfect and finite—which itself is the evidence (proof) that a perfect and infinite other (God) exists. Spinoza alters Descartes's "I think therefore I am" to "I am as I think [*ego sum cogitans*]," noting that it was not a proof (syllogism). Likewise, Descartes's proof of the existence of God is not, in fact, a proof in the strict sense of the word. Descartes wanted to say that even if there is no basis for him to be outside the community as a singularity—as he was—there must still be something that prompts him to be, and because this something exists, he doubts. Expressed more concretely, this "something" designates precisely the fact that there are other communities, or others who follow different sets of rules.

"Spirit" for Descartes meant not simply "to think," but "to doubt" if this thinking amounted only to "obeying the rules of a community." Though this is tantamount to an attempt to move to a position external to the community, Descartes himself did not understand this to be the case. Rather, this exteriority came to be interiorized in Cartesianism; that is, "thinking" itself came to be taken for "spirit," and simultaneously the otherness/difference that had shadowed Cartesian doubt was erased. One of Descartes's most important early critics was Spinoza, who, paradoxically, had attempted to further develop Cartesianism. For Spinoza God is coextensive with the world. Far from being beyond this world, the Cartesian ideas "free will" and "God" are sheer representations produced within this world. Even so, Spinoza resisted belonging to any single community. He was a singular *cogito* and an external existence. Singularity is, in this exact sense, social.

Paul Valéry said that the *cogito* is another name for Descartes, implying that Descartes's singularity is irrelevant to the individuality or self that is applicable to all. To turn this around, we could say that Michel Foucault is another *cogito;* yet as soon as Foucault's beliefs are accepted, the same thing that occurred with Cartesianism would occur again with Foucaultianism. One could, without reservations, criticize Cartesianism along the lines of Foucault's challenge. It is this pattern that dominates today's discourses. At present, calling attention to the precedence of language or community has itself become institutionalized.

Author's Note

As a postscript to this chapter, I would like to add a few remarks on Kant. There is no doubt that Kant criticized the Cartesian *cogito ergo sum* as a parallogism, and further argued that the *cogito* was merely "a transcendental subject of thought = X," incidental to the speculative function of any origin. Husserl attempted to locate the problematic of the transcendental subject in Descartes and *not* in Kant. But it was Kant who elaborated on the concept of the "transcendental" in contradistinction to "transcendent." Thus, if Kant lacked the "transcendental subject" in the Husserlian sense, neither did it exist in Descartes. *Cogito ergo sum*, as I have shown previously, is both a consciousness of difference and an external existence; therefore, once it loses differentiality/externality and is constituted as a positive term, it will turn into a psychological ego, or a transcendental ego that has a tendency to continually constitute the world. This is exactly what happened with Descartes. Spinoza offered this critique: by proposing that world equals nature equals god, he suggested that the subject that composes the world is merely an imaginary reflection within the world. This was less a denial of the *cogito* than its radicalization to the extremities of differentiation and externality. In fact, the problematic of *cogito* is embodied, paradoxically, in those thinkers who never addressed it, or even denied it. The Kantian *cogito* cannot be found in the subjectivity that constructs the world, but in the very stance of his "transcendental critique"—that which can never be constituted as a positive term.

What Kant named the "thing-in-itself" corresponds to Spinoza's world equals nature. While it affects the human via the sensible, it can only be represented as *Schein* (semblance). Kant erected the "transcendental" as opposed to the "transcendent" as a critique of that which presumes to grasp the "thing-in-itself." This distinguishes Kant's "transcendental critique" from Husserl's "transcendental phenomenology," which is content with finding universal reason at the foundation of the "life-world." The "transcendental critique" for Kant is a query, not of content but of recognition itself: it consists of bracketing that which we empirically take for granted as "natural," and scrutinizing the formal conditions that enable such a fictive construct to take hold in the mind—the community. Yet, in the final analysis, it is the difference between discursive systems that makes it possible at all, as in the case of the Cartesian *cogito*.

After criticizing/scrutinizing the individual realms of the faculties in human recognition—"our cognitive faculties," "the faculty of desire," and "the feeling of pleasure or displeasure"—Kant declared that this "critique" itself did not belong to any of these categories. Under which realm, then, does this critique of reason by reason—the transcendental critique—fall? It belongs nowhere other than to a *topos* of difference. It is misleading to speak of this *locus* in terms of a concrete spatiality, yet it is inseparable from the physical locality of Kant's life in Königsberg. It is well known that he rarely left this town during his lifetime, refusing, in particular, to go to Berlin, the political capital of the region. Though politically unimportant, Königsberg, active port on the Baltic, was not a provincial town but a center of communication, supplied with information from various resources. It reminds one of the role of Amsterdam for Descartes. Kant "lived" the *cogito*.

It was inappropriate for Husserl to claim that Kant had lost sight of the problematic of the transcendental subjectivity that had been grasped so firmly by Descartes. Furthermore, it seems necessary to free the meaning of the term "transcendental" from the restriction of the Husserlian framework. "Transcendental" identifies a stance of doubting the apodictic discursive space in which we are entrapped, while simultaneously questioning the "inversion" constantly at work in this space. Seen in this light, Nietzsche's "genealogy," and indeed the critical projects of Marx and Freud, can also be called transcendental critiques.

It can be said that Meno's paradox, which asserts that neither teaching nor learning is possible, reveals, conversely, that every communication tacitly assumes the teaching-learning relationship as a basic condition. Let us remember that Socrates appears to be a teacher in all of Plato's "dialogues." His teaching position notwithstanding, the asymmetrical teaching-learning relationship is discreetly replaced in the dialogue by the symmetrical relationship of "seeking the truth in company." With respect to the "recollection"—this method for "seeking in company"—we must turn to Freudian psychoanalysis, in which a therapeutic treatment is effected in the "recollection" through "dialogue." Like Socrates, a psychoanalyst does not teach anything but simply helps the patient to recall; the dialogue is driven by the patient's identification with or transference to the doctor.

Yet psychoanalysis is quite distinct from Plato's dialogue. In Freud, therapy is terminated only with the *removal* of the patient's transference to the doctor. While Plato approached an erotic synthesis, Freud intended to sustain the asymmetrical doctor-patient relationship. More to the point, in Freudian analysis, "recollection" always involves the revelation of the asymmetry of relation. As opposed to Plato's recollection—which aims at the "common essence"—the

Freudian approach is to recollect what is repressed by and hidden under the "common essence" or "symmetrical relationship." Inasmuch as repression is always the interiorization of otherness, recollection of this sort is aimed at a revelation of the repressed. What Freud called the Oedipus complex is, as it were, the interiorization of the other (father) and a symmetrization of the asymmetrical relationship between father and child.

What is even more crucial is that Freud showed that the Unconscious exists only in the asymmetrical relationship with the other: the Unconscious exists for neither the patient nor doctor alone, but only for the relationship between doctor and patient; it exists only in the patient's *denial* (resistance). In Freud knowledge never relinquishes its hold on this relationship with the other; in this sense Freud's methodology distinguishes itself from phenomenological (introspective) approaches. In the Freudian context the other subsumes even the other who, being totally *indifferent*, neither transfers to nor resists the doctor. In our context, the essence of the otherness of the other lies in this very indifference.

I promised to make you understand by the help of the fact of transference why our therapeutic efforts have no success with the narcissistic neuroses. . . . Observation shows that sufferers from narcissistic neuroses have no capacity for transference or only insufficient residues of it. They reject the doctor, not with hostility but with indifference. For that reason they cannot be influenced by him either; what he says leaves them cold, makes no impression on them; consequently the mechanism of cure which we carry through with other people—the revival of the pathogenic conflict and the overcoming of the resistance due to repression—cannot be operated with them. They remain as they are. Often they have already undertaken attempts at recovery on their own account which have led to pathological results. We cannot alter this in any way. . . . They manifest no transference and for that reason are inaccessible to our efforts and cannot be cured by us.[1]

Here we see Freud's acknowledgment of the limitation of psychoanalysis. However, this does not indicate incompetence: Freudian psychoanalysis does not give up a recognition of the other that cannot be included within the self. (It might be pointed out, however, that innumerable psychopathologies operate on the presupposition of "transference," a symmetrical relationship.) Freud thus offers a radical critique of the presupposition of a symmetrical relationship between self and other. Psychoanalytic knowledge cannot exist if is separated from the actual "dialogic" relationship, and therefore is not universally applicable through a certain theorization. Many, including Karl Popper, have attacked psychoanalysis as not scientific; this is because it radically questions the canonical notion of the "dialogue" that is understood to be the basis of science.

It is curious that Freud thought it imperative to charge his patients high prices in order to have them periodically "recall" that the terms of their relationship were not of a familiar but of a business nature. In a therapeutic turn that has potentially negative consequences for the doctor, the cure is complete only when the patients begin to see the doctor as simply a doctor, thereby distancing themselves from the doctor. This situation is quite unlike that of Socrates, who, unlike other Sophists, did not charge anything for his services, and who therefore erased the asymmetrical teaching-learning relationship. Freud, on the other hand, charged a fee in order to maintain the relation of asymmetry.

Money is not just another part of therapy. Psychoanalysts earn their living by their labor: it is not because doctors charge that patients are cured, but rather that patients are cured so that doctors can profit. It is strange that this aspect of money is overlooked. Moreover, Freud took the same position toward his disciples as Socrates took toward his: he did not charge them for his educational analysis, and this charge-free relationship ultimately formed an esoteric cluster of erotic identification.

What ground is created in this exchange (equation) between therapy as labor and money? As Marx held, the exchange is ungrounded. "They do this without being aware of it."[2] This sort of "unconsciousness" exists outside the domain of psychoanalysis. For this reason, Marx's theory of the "form of value" should not be interpreted as it was by the Lacanian school of psychoanalysis. The asymmetrical relationship of selling-buying shadows every field or domain of inquiry—art, science, religion. Any thought that despises *secularness*, or the asymmetrical relationship, is absorbed into metaphysics. In the diary written near the end of his life, Kierkegaard expressed his surprise that he received royalties from the sale of his books. This *surprise* masks an issue that is equally important to those he wrote about in those books. Although connected with the relative other "without being aware of it," Kierkegaard, who died just when his inheritance was used up, did not have to ponder this problem.

For Aristotle there was no common value immanent in the commodity, and thus no rational basis in exchange. Exchange was for him just "a makeshift for practical purposes."[3] Marx praised Aristotle for recognizing the "form of value" when the classical economists could not. Regarding Aristotle, Marx writes, "In the first place, he states quite clearly that the money-form of the commodity is only a more developed aspect of the simple form of value, i.e. of the expression of the value of a commodity in some other commodity chosen at random."[4] Aristotle was able to say this, however, only because he despised commerce. For Aristotle, only philosophy could discover the identical essence (*idea*); but, like Plato, he thought that this identity could be discovered as an identification. Plato maintained that "there is no such thing as teaching." Classical economics repeated this on a different level: commodities are exchangeable because of their common essence, and thus selling equals buying. This amounts to saying that there is no such thing as *selling*.

From our vantage point, selling and buying are completely distinct affairs. Marx shows the simple form of value as follows.

$$20 \text{ yards of linen} = 1 \text{ coat}$$
(the relative form of value)   (the equivalent form)

This equation, which assumes a kind of life among the commodities, proposes that the value of 20 yards of linen, being unable to express its value by itself, has no other choice than to be expressed in its natural form, but only after first being equated with a coat; a coat, on the other hand, is always in a position to be exchanged with the former. The secret of Marx's analysis of the fetishism of commodity lies in this equivalent form—it is that which disguises a coat as if it contained an immanent value within itself. "The equivalent form of a commodity, accordingly, is the form in which it is directly exchangeable with other commodities."[5] To put it differently, the relative form of value represents the "standpoint of selling" and the equivalent form represents the "standpoint of buying." The simple form of value can thus be seen as the condensation of the asymmetrical relationship of "selling-buying." "The relative form of value and the equivalent form are two inseparable moments, which belong to and mutually condition each other; but, at the same time, they are mutually exclusive or opposed extremes, i.e. poles of the expression of value."[6]

In this simple equation, a coat is not always the equivalent form, because 20 yards of linen, too, can take the position of an equivalent form.

Of course, the expression 20 yards of linen = 1 coat, or 20 yards of linen are worth 1 coat, also includes its converse: 1 coat = 20 yards of linen, or 1 coat is worth 20 yards of linen. But in this case I must reverse the equation, in order to express the value of the coat relatively; and, if I do that, the linen becomes the equivalent instead of the coat. The same commodity cannot, therefore, simultaneously appear in both forms in the same expression of value. These forms rather exclude each other as polar opposites.

Whether a commodity is in the relative form or in its opposite, the equivalent form, entirely depends on its actual position in the expression of value. That is, it depends on whether it is the commodity whose value is being expressed, or the commodity in which value is being expressed.[7]

At this point either could emerge as the equivalent form—this implies the crucial fact that the owner of each commodity intends to take the position of buying and avoid the position of selling. Marx details the "development" from the simple form of value to the general form of value in which a special commodity exclusively occupies the equivalent form, prompting every other commodity to become a relative form of value. Perhaps it is not necessary to follow this development in such detail, though it is important to stress in particular one point: although this description resembles a Hegelian "development," Marx actually recurs via genealogical retrospection to the simple form of value, which more developed forms come to conceal.

Hence the mysteriousness of the equivalent form, which only impinges on the crude bourgeois vision of the political economist when it confronts him in its fully developed shape, that of money. He then seeks to explain away the mystical character of gold and silver by substituting for them less dazzling commodities, and, with ever-renewed satisfaction, reeling off a catalogue of all the inferior commodities which have played the role of the equivalent at one time or another. He does not suspect that even the simplest expression of value, such as 20 yards of linen = 1 coat, already presents the riddle of the equivalent form for us to solve.[8]

The simple form of value illustrates several things. First, it is not on account of its inherent nature that a certain thing becomes an equivalent form. For example, gold can be an equivalent form or money not because it is *gold* but because it becomes the equivalent form. The Monetarists believed that the secret of gold's use as money lay in its peculiarity. However, gold is special only because it is posited in the money form and *not vice versa*; this becomes clear when we consider the fact that a piece of paper by itself is legal tender. That piece of paper becomes money only insofar as it is becomes the equivalent form.

It is in the Monetary System that the fetishism of money can most clearly be observed. Marx's objective was not to criticize the illusory nature of money; this had already been accomplished by the classical economists, for whom money was either a measure of the immanent value (labor time) of a commodity or a means of circulation. They regarded the production of goods as the most important aspect of the economy, and, in turn, overlooked the fact that "mysteriousness" is important as the essential motive power inherent in capitalism. Moreover, classical economics lost sight of the asymmetrical relationship between *capital*—the standpoint of buying—and *wage workers*, who, with only their labor as commodity, are always obliged to assume the position of selling. Classical economics thus overlooked completely the "crisis" caused by the very sine qua non of capital: in order to sustain its self-increase, capital must stand in the selling position at least once.

For Marx to criticize the fetishism of money was not enough because, to repeat, money had already been *demystified* in classical economics. He emphasized, instead, the fetishism of the commodity. "The riddle of the money fetish is therefore the riddle of the commodity fetish, now become visible and dazzling to our eyes."[9] It was in order to extract the essential asymmetrical relationship of selling-buying that Marx stressed the precedence of the commodity fetish. No matter how it proceeds, capitalist development will never be able to sublate this asymmetrical relationship, but can only manage to conceal it.[10]

Marx's theoretical framework owes a great deal to classical economics. In his "critique" of political economy, Marx reappraises issues that belonged to *pre*-classical economics—the inherently problematic nature of merchant capitalism. Marx's appreciation of Aristotle offers a good example:

Where did the illusions of the Monetary System come from? The adherents of the Monetary System did not see gold and silver as representing money as a social relation of production, but in the form of natural objects with peculiar social properties. And what of modern political economy, which looks down so disdainfully on the Monetary System? Does not its fetishism become quite palpable when it deals with capital? How long is it since the disappearance of the Physiocratic illusion that ground rent grows out of the soil, not out of society?[1]

In the above citation, Marx does not simply scorn the illusory nature of the Monetary System. During the crises that periodically recurred during the age of classical economics, the phenomenon of abandoning commodities in favor of money was not an "illusion" but a fact. The classical economists regarded this reality as accidental and laughed at the "illusion" that caused people to turn to money. People turn to money because it is the general equivalent form that offers direct exchangeability. This fetishism of money is expressed in our desire to avoid the selling position— that is, subordinating ourselves to the will of others— and, instead, to seek the position from which we can exchange directly at any time.

Marx's theory of the value form was an attempt to reassess the fetishism of money that classical economists looked down upon so disdainfully. Rather than attempting to illustrate how the value form of the commodity developed into the money form, Marx instead wanted to reveal the asymmetry in the commodity-money or selling-buying relation at its most fundamental level. He did this through what could be called *genealogical retrospection*. The "development" of the value form functions instead as a concealment of the fundamental asymmetry. To repeat, money was ignored by classical economics. This indifference corresponds to classical economists' denial of the previous mercantilism and their emphasis on industrial capital as essentially different from mercantile capital. Thus the value of the commodity is understood in terms of the human labor contained in an object and is expressed as a relation of social "labor time"; the equivalent exchange of the commodity is unquestioned, while the fact that surplus value (profit) is gained in the *difference* (unequivalent exchange) is omitted. The driving force of capitalism then is the production of materials (property or use value); accordingly, the *motive* to hoard gold (money) is rejected as unethical and morbid.

Departing from this kind of analysis, Marx analyzed industrial capital by returning to the problems of merchant capital. Whether industrial or merchant, capital itself has the same motivation. But it is irrelevant to the desire to accumulate property.[2] For though it is the case that merchant and industrial capital are different, emphasizing their differences prevents us from understanding the true nature of capitalism.

What Marx said with respect to circulation is summarized as follows: in the process of circulation C–M–C (commodity–money–commodity), C–M (selling) and M–C (buying) are separate, and hence, unlike in the direct exchange of products C–C, the sphere of exchange is infinitely expandable in both space and time. Nevertheless, because of the "fatal leap" implicit in C–M, which should then be more accurately schematized as $C,-M$, the "possibility of crises" is omnipresent. If circulation is expressed in the cycle C–M–C, this process simultaneously contains the process in reverse M–C as well as $C,-M$. (Note: the process in reverse is not M–C–M.) That is to say, the movement of money is actually the circulation of commodities, but *not vice versa*. "Hence although the movement of money is merely the expression of the circulation of commodities, the situation appears to be the reverse of this, namely the circulation of commodities seems to be the result of the movement of money."[3] The movements of C–M–C and M–C–M seem like the front and back of the same cycle, though they are completely different because the initiative of the circulation is seized totally by the hand of money (owner).

Simply expressed, the movement of capital is M–C–M, (M + ΔM). As our viewpoint shifts, the cycle appears as a circulation more of the commodity than of money, and therefore the movement of capital is concealed within the circulation of commodity. It is in this way that the self-movement of capital in classical economics was understood to be already dissolved within the circulation of commodities or in the tautological circuit of *production of property* or *process of consumption*. However, implicit in the economic phenomena that appear merely as "production of property and consumption," there exists a perverted drive that is irrelevant to them: the fetishism of money.

Indeed, as Marx proclaimed, merchant capital develops "in between" communities, fertilized by the difference between various systems of values. For that matter, industrial capital, too, profits (gains surplus value) from the same difference, without which it could not even be capital (self-increasing money). But while merchant capital gains surplus value *spatially*—from the difference between various systems of values—industrial capital gains excessive profit (relative surplus value) *temporally*, by an incessant differentiation of the value system organized by technology. This does not mean that industrial capital cannot be profitable at the same time that temporal difference as merchant capital does. Surplus value may be achieved by any means whatsoever.

In my previous book on Marx, I demonstrated that the self-movement of capital could be explained without relying on the concept of labor time.[4] What I would like to focus on in this chapter, however, is less a question of how the self-increase of capital is made possible than of why the movement of capital endures. Even before the emergence of industrial capital, the entire capitalist apparatus was already in place; industrial capital simply adapted this apparatus to its own needs. What, then, is this "perversion" that motivates the capitalist movement of the economy? Obviously, it is money, or, more to the point, it is the fetishism of commodity.

At the fountainhead of merchant capital Marx discovered a *miser* who actually lives this fetishism of money. Owning money amounts to owning "social privilege," by means of which one can exchange anything, anytime, anywhere. A miser (money hoarder) is a person who gives up the actual use value in exchange for this "right." The impulse to hoard money, treating it not as a medium but as a thing to be desired for its own sake, derives not from a material need; on the contrary, the miser, just like the *dévot* who is indifferent to this world in order to "accumulate riches in heaven," is not interested in materiality. In misers one finds a quality akin to religious fanaticism. Indeed, both money saving (hoarding) and world religion appeared as soon as circulation—which was first formed "in between" communities and gradually interiorized within them—became global. The same sublime perversion appears in the religious and the miser. Whether mediated by the desire of others or not, the motive for saving money does not come from a desire for material (use value). Psychological or physiological approaches to analyzing this motive are altogether more vulgar than the miser himself, because what truly informs the motives of the miser is a *religious* problematic.

The miserly desire is thus motivated by an attempt to avoid the position of selling, an attempt, in other words, to remain in the buying position. In reality, one no sooner buys than one is forced to assume the position of selling. What is required, then, is a sustained occupation of the buying position. The fetishism of money is thus most typically embodied in the miser who attempts to save money; or rather, the saving itself is generated by the miser's fetishism of money. For if money is saved, material can be purchased anytime; there is no need to stockpile. That is to say, saving itself begins as a saving of money. There has never been an autotelic impulse to save in any "community" outside the sphere of the currency economy. As Georges Bataille put it, in such communities, excessive products are wasted.

Far from being driven by need or desire, saving is rooted in the perversion that is totally opposed to it—it is the saving that creates in us a more-than-necessary need and multifarious desire. To be sure, the savings of the miser and those of the capitalist are not the same; while the miser attempts to be left out of the circulation process by "selling more and buying less," the capitalist has to voluntarily leap into the self-movement M–C–M, $(M + \Delta M)$.

Use-values must therefore never be treated as the immediate aim of the capitalist; nor must the profit on any single transaction. His aim is rather the unceasing movement of profit-making. The boundless drive for enrichment, this passionate chase after value, is common to the capitalist and the miser; but while the miser is merely a capitalist gone mad, the capitalist is a rational miser. The ceaseless augmentation of value, which the miser seeks to attain by saving his money from circulation, is achieved by the more acute capitalist by means of throwing his money again and again into circulation.[5]

The motivation for the movement of merchant capital is the same as the saving impulse (money fetishism) of a miser. Saving money for merchant capital is a saving of material, though it appears less as an accumulation of various products from various places than as an expansion of the circulation process or of the processes of production and consumption. The same can be said about industrial capital—it does not aim at the increase of property (use value), as classical economics thought. In this sense, it is appropriate that with regard to the motive of industrial capital, Max Weber proposed an *ascetic* response to use value. Puritans were rational misers, as it were; however, what drives capitalism is not their rationality but their perversion. This attempt to avoid the selling position in exchange, after all, functions as a motive force for the further expansion of exchange.

It is not the primary objective of this study to focus on
the entire workings of capitalism. What is crucial to
observe is that the movement of capital is rooted in
a certain perversion that compels its movement.
To understand this aspect of the movement of
capital, it is necessary to reflect upon credit.
The movement of capital must go through
the cycle C–M (selling), which the miser
most fears and wishes to avoid, because if
the cycle is not completed, the movement will come to a halt with a loss of
money, with only material as a
result: M = C. To temporarily   *Twenty-one* **Credit**
avoid this danger, it is necessary
to resort to credit. According
to Marx's rhetoric, this is to
assume the selling (C–M)
ideally, in advance; credit
takes the form of exchange
where, though the actual payment is temporarily suspended,
the counterbalancing/settling of
accounts will occur later. Of course
a bank note (or a check) is credit, and,
for that matter, money is itself already a
kind of credit.

Economic anthropology—a field that
understands the origin of money as a religious event—criticizes Marx's viewpoint as
modernist. What Marx argued, however, is that
there is no rational ground in the exchange—
understood in this way, exchange does not necessarily contradict Bataille's "general economics" of
gift and counter-gift. How, in a primitive barter system, can two products generated in different seasons be

exchanged? The party who has been the recipient of gift A will later reciprocate with the return of B. In some native peoples' mind, this event is narrated through a representation: because a certain magical power (*mana*) is contained in A, they will be cursed unless they make a return, B; in this manner it appears as if the gift formed an exchange. On the contrary, it can also be argued that the need to exchange simply takes the form of a gift. Marx noted that in the process of exchange "they do this without being aware of it"; it is important that this statement also implies that humans are *aware* of it in different ways. There is no rational ground for any exchange, whether uncivilized or modern. By insisting on the priority of the exchange rather than that of the gift, it is possible to say that even in an exchange with money as a means of payment, money contains a *mana*-like (social, compulsory) power: this is exactly what we call "credit." Moreover, money can take any form whatsoever inasmuch as credit resides in it. For that reason, a simple piece of paper (such as a check or bank note) commands a restraining power.

As Marx observed, the institution of credit, having come into existence together with the expansion of circulation in a *naturwüchsiges* manner, expands circulation itself. A credit system accelerates and eternalizes the cycle of capital movement, for with this system capitalists can begin new investments without having to wait for the outcome of the cycle M–C–M. However, the fact that the origin of credit is *naturwüchsiges* means it does not have a rational ground. Credit is not formed within a state or a community, but "in between" them, in the "social" relationship. No political power is free to design and construct a credit system as it wishes; it can only give legal support to the credit system, because it is actually the political power itself that relies on the social credit system.

The essence of credit lies in its avoidance of the crisis inherent in the selling position—the postponement of the present crisis to some future date. Though the balance must eventually be paid with money, it can always be deferred. This temporal postponement in a sense reverses the movement of capital M–C–M. The instability of the selling position may not surface immediately; because of the nature of credit, it appears as if the sale were already made. The danger is metamorphosed into the uncertainty of future money payment. Under the credit system, then, the self-movement of capital occurs not so much because of its desire for saving, but because of its desperate need to postpone the settlement indefinitely. From this moment on, the self-movement of capital surpasses the will of individual capitalists and becomes a compulsion.

Credit enforces capital movement indefinitely at the same time that it hastens the self-increase of capital and eliminates the danger involved in *selling*. Seen in aggregate, the self-movement of capital must endure the indefinite postponement of the *settlement* as a stopgap maneuver. It was previously pointed out that the movement of capital demands an incessant differentiation in order to ensure difference (surplus value); in this context, it implies that instead of technological innovation being caused by the ideology of progress, the ideology of progress is itself generated as a result of the movement of capital. However, if considered from the vantage point of credit, the movement of capital is no longer simply a necessity for profit making, but is compelled by the necessity of settlement. The *temporality* of capitalism manifest in a process of constant differentiation is by no means an advance toward the *infinite* future, but an incessant deferment of the settlement to the *indefinite* future.

To be sure, from time to time the moment of settlement comes as a surprise attack: this is the crisis that appears—only where credit is fully developed—as nothing short of a collapse of credit. Nevertheless, credit is neither a mere illusion nor an ideology. Even if there is a certain truth in the assertion that the currency economy forms an *illusory* system, it is still true that the *real* that people encounter, once this *illusion* collapses, is nothing natural. It is money.

Such a crisis occurs only where the ongoing chain of payments has been fully developed, along with an artificial system for settling them. Whenever there is a general disturbance of the mechanism, no matter what its cause, money suddenly and immediately changes over from its merely nominal shape, money of account, into hard cash. Profane commodities can no longer replace it. The use-value of commodities becomes valueless, and their value vanishes in the face of their own form of value. The bourgeois, drunk with prosperity and arrogantly certain of himself, has just declared that money is a purely imaginary creation. "Commodities alone are money," he said. But now the opposite cry resounds over the markets of the world: only money is a commodity. As the heart pants after fresh water, so pants his soul after money, the only wealth. In a crisis, the antithesis between commodities and their value-form, money, is raised to the level of an absolute contradiction. Hence money's form of appearance is here also a matter of indifference. The monetary famine remains whether payments have to be made in gold or in credit-money, such as bank-notes.[1]

In times of crisis it is not the material form of the commodity that people cling to, but the "direct exchangeability" (equivalent form) of the commodity—money itself. By means of a kind of psychoanalytic retrospection, Marx read the crisis as a symptom and diagnosed the fundamental illness of capitalism in its inherent asymmetrical relationship. The object of Marx's analysis is thus a classical crisis. But this illness is not a sign of the radical collapse of capitalism but, more properly, a part of the whole process of the prosperity cycle (prosperity–crisis–depression–prosperity). The crisis and the depression that follows are merely parts of the violent (liberalistic) reformation of capitalist production itself. It is pointless, however, to think that the main defect of capitalism lies in this inevitability of depression—that the problem will be solved if the prosperity cycle is "consciously" administered. No matter what political result it may cause, a crisis is not the sign of the collapse of capitalism but a part of its whole cycle.

As might be evident already, the economic process is not the same as the so-called infrastructure. It is rather a religious process in which the end is indefinitely deferred. And whether it is one of capitalism or religion, the real crisis is in exchange or communication with the other. Whether economic, religious, or other, any critique of metaphysics that attempts to dissolve the crisis within its theoretical mechanism is thus equally indispensable. Kierkegaard criticized Hegel for having dissolved religion into philosophy. According to Hegel, Christ is God incarnated as a man—which means that man is God. It is at this moment that the criticism of Christianity by the Hegelian *die Linke* began. For Feuerbach God is self-alienation of the "generic essence" inherent in individuals. This logic is isomorphic to Marx's early critique of classical economics, in which he suggested that money is a self-alienation of the common essence (labor) implicit in individual commodities.

If classical economics is equivalent to Hegelian philosophy, then Marx's critique of the former can be seen to correspond to Kierkegaard's critique of the latter. Hegel exercised an ex post facto proof (rationalization) stating that, since Christianity developed historically,

Christ was God. In contrast, Kierkegaard stressed that it was important to "contemporaneously" confront Christ as God, appearing in all of his "lowliness." What is important to note here, however, is that there is no ground that we can appeal to in order to acknowledge Christ as God; to acknowledge this requires a "leap" or a "leap in the dark." As Kierkegaard writes: "Christendom has abolished Christianity without really knowing it itself. As a result, if something must be done, one must attempt again to introduce Christianity into Christendom."[2]

Money appears in all of its "lowliness," yet one repeats the "fatal leap" in order to obtain it; this fact notwithstanding, everyone regards it merely as a means of indicating the value of a commodity. Marx's critique of classical economics can be understood by rewriting Kierkegaard's expression: "The Currency economy has abolished Currency without really knowing it itself. As a result, if something must be done, one must attempt again to introduce Currency into the Currency economy." In other words it is necessary to observe the crisis—the asymmetrical relationship that cannot be sublated—immanent in C–M (selling).

What is more, the temporality of capitalism is similar to that of Judeo-Christianity insofar as both are indefinitely deferred. What I would like to stress by such an analogy, however, is neither parallelism nor correlativity between religious and economic phenomena. For whether or not we believe in religion, capitalism situates us in a structure similar to that of religion. What motivates us is not *idea*, realistic need, or desire; it is rather a metaphysics and a theology inscribed in the form of the commodity itself, rooted in the ungroundedness and crisis immanent in our communication and exchange. Marx's real achievement in *Capital* is a radical critique of modes of thought that sought to dissolve the "other." It is crucial to note that this other is *not* an absolute but a vulgar other, which, because of its vulgarness, can never be dissolved by any type of absolute *idea* whatsoever. Marx thus revealed an *absoluteness* of the "relative relationship."

To put it simply, the movement of capital socially connects people from all over the world. Yet because this sociality is mediational, we are not conscious of it. Though we are actually connected to each other, we are unaware of it. Some ideologues in advanced nations argue that, for example, the class struggle is a mere fiction of the modern age; they insist instead on the reconstruction of reason by "dialogue." These are *fictions* made possible, of course, by the imposition of their own rules onto the people of the Third World. Irrespective of these fictions and ideologies, it is finally impossible to argue against the absolute certainty of the relations that factually exist.

Having come into existence together with the "world market" that was consolidated by the merchant and industrial capitalist movements, Hegel's "world history" was retrospectively reconstructed. Woven by the movement of capital, our history has no Hegelian end or *telos*, because, as we have seen, the end is indefinitely deferred. It is concerning this aspect of our world that Marx wrote the following: "Communism is for us not a *state of affairs* which is to be established, an *ideal* to which reality [will] have to adjust itself. We call communism the *real* movement which abolishes [*aufhebt*] the present state of things. The conditions of this movement result from the premises now in existence."[3] The interminable movement of capital dismantles any fiction that presupposes an end. The "*real* movement which abolishes [*aufhebt*] the present state of things," which Marx grasped, is not that which can be planned in advance, but what always happens as a surprise attack.

Today's debates on postmodernism are fundamentally critiques of the narrative of the Hegelian *Idee*. For Hegel world history is a self-realization of *Idee*, and for many, Marxism is a mere variant of it. Is it possible that what has taken place since 1989 is the disintegration of the *Idee*? I think not. Instead a new kind of Hegelian *Idee* of world history, this time manifest as the "end of history," has emerged: achieved enlightenment, entitled "communicative rationality," and a cynicism that scorns any *Idee* (only because it has been harmed by it). While "the end of history" is proclaimed in the advanced nation-states of the Northern Hemisphere, in the Southern Hemisphere various religious fundamentalisms are becoming more and more active. It is in this context that the reassessment of *Idee* becomes urgent. For Kant, who borrowed his concept from Plato, *Idee* is an imaginary representation of the "thing-in-itself": it is that which can never be grasped and represented by any theoretical approach. However, what is important is that the concept of the "thing-in-itself" was proposed by Kant less as an account of the true world, as with Plato's *idea*, than as the basis upon which to criticize all the ideation as *Schein*. Moreover, Kant did not simplemindedly deny *Idee*: he claimed, after all, that *Idee* was a necessary *Schein* that functions "regulatively," though it cannot be

proven theoretically and must never be realized "constitutively." After Kant, the "thing-in-itself" was generally
ignored by philosophers, whereupon emerged the
Hegelian position that *Idee* is realistic and the real is
ideation. No matter how materialistic he appeared to be,
Marx, in his early career, still belonged within this
Hegelian system. "Philosophy cannot realize itself without the transcendence [*Aufhebung*] of the proletariat, and
the proletariat cannot transcend itself without the realization [*Verwirklichung*] of philosophy."[1] This phrase
implies a causality in which philosophy (*Idee*) is realistic
and the real (proletariat) is ideation.

By comparison, beginning with *The German
Ideology*, Marx's critique of Hegel makes a radical departure from this materialistic reversal; while Althusser
called it an "epistemological break," it is, on my view, a
return to the Kantian "transcendental critique." By seeing the philosophical discourses of the Hegelian *die
Linke* (including Marx's own) from outside of Germany,
The German Ideology revealed these Hegelian discourses
to be merely *Schein*. Moreover, Marx showed that all
discourses are possible only as a *Schein*: this was made
possible by positing history as the "thing-in-itself." And
this history is the "*naturwüchsiges* manifold," unstruc-
turable by any form whatsoever. Marx rejected the
"spirit" and "transcendental ego" that integrate it into
the imaginary.

Marx did not deny the *Idee* unconditionally.
Instead, he acknowledged that it had a certain
inevitability, even granting that, theoretically, it was
Schein. What he did deny was the "constitutive" function of *Idee*; he consistently criticized the "constitutive"
program for the development of a future society. It
must be noted that in his entire corpus Marx only rarely
dealt with a program for the future: in *The Manifesto of*

the Communist Party, which was a collaboration with Engels, and in *Critique of the Gotha Programme*, which was written simply as a critical commentary on someone else's program.

Marx persisted in criticizing the "constitutive" use of reason, a kind of reason put into practice by the communism initiated at the Russian Revolution. Communism's collapse, however, has not led to the total disintegration of *Idee*, because *Idee* is, from the beginning, merely a *Schein*. And whatever kinds of *Idee* are preached as substitutes, they too are mere *Schein*. To repeat, Marx acknowledged the need and inevitability of *Idee*. Even in the early *Critique of Hegel's Philosophy of Right* Marx differed with both Feuerbach and the Hegelian *die Linke*; this phrase is well known, but often misinterpreted:

Religious suffering is at one and the same time the *expression* of real suffering and a protest against real suffering. Religion is the sigh of the oppressed creature, the heart of a heartless world and the soul of soulless conditions. It is the *opium* of the people.

The abolition of religion as the *illusory* happiness of the people is the demand for their *real* happiness. To call on them to give up their illusions about their condition is to *call on them to give up a condition that requires illusions.* The criticism of religion is therefore in *embryo* the *criticism of that vale of tears* of which religion is the halo.[2]

Marx attempts to say that it is impossible to dissolve any religion unless the "real suffering" upon which every religion is based is dissolved. There is no reason to criticize religion theoretically, because it can only be dissolved practically. While philosophers of the Enlightenment criticize religion through reason, such a "*criticism of religion* has been essentially completed."[3]

Religion, albeit as *Schein*, has a certain necessity inasmuch as man is an existence of passivity (pathos); it functions "regulatively" as a protest against reality, if not a "constitution" of reality.

Although communism as well is a mere *Schein*, to criticize its "illusion" means no more and no less than "to call on [people] to give up a condition that requires illusions." And religion will be upheld so long as this state of affairs endures. We can never dissolve fundamentalism by the criticisms or dialogues motivated by enlightenment, precisely because to criticize the "illusion" of the latter is "to call on them to give up a condition that requires illusions." The advocating of the collapse of *Idee* and the insistence on its realization are, in fact, intertwined and inseparable, and both are *Schein* that represent, each in its own way, the real (the thing-in-itself) of world capitalism, of which they themselves are members.

Introduction to the English Edition

1. Plato, *The Symposium*, trans. Walter Hamilton (Harmondsworth, England: Penguin, 1951), 85.

   Translator's note: In as many as three English translations of the text, *poiesis* is translated as poetry; however, to be more precise and to accord with the context in the current volume, I have replaced "poetry" and "poets" with [*poiesis*] and [creators].

2. See Edmund Husserl, *L'origine de la géométrie*, translated with an introduction by Jacques Derrida, Epiméthée, Essais Philosophiques, Collection fondeé par Jean Hyppolite (Paris: Presses Universitaires, 1962). English translation: Jacques Derrida, *Edmund Husserl's "Origin of Geometry": An Introduction*, trans. John P. Leavey, Jr. (Lincoln: University of Nebraska Press, 1962).

3. Karl Marx and Friedrich Engels, *The German Ideology, Part One*, ed. C. J. Arthur (New York: International Publishers, 1947), 54.

4. Edward W. Said, *The World, the Text, and the Critic* (Cambridge, Mass.: Harvard University Press, 1983), 3–4.

5. Ludwig F. Wittgenstein, *Remarks on the Foundations of Mathematics*, ed. G. H. von Wright, R. Rhees, and G. E. M. Anscombe, trans. G. E. M. Anscombe (Cambridge, Mass.: MIT Press, 1978), 383.

6. Ludwig F. Wittgenstein, *Philosophical Investigations*, 2d ed., trans. G. E. M. Anscombe (New York: Macmillan, 1958), 39e.

7. Many philosophers after Kant, however, did omit the "thing-in-itself"; hence the advent of the Hegelian stance that insists that *Idee* (*idea*) is realistic and the real is ideatic.

8. Immanuel Kant, *Critique of Aesthetic Judgement*, trans. James Creed Meredith (Oxford: Clarendon Press, 1911), 5.

One **The Will to Architecture**

1. Plato, *The Symposium.* See also note 1 in the Introduction to the English Edition, above.

2. Francis MacDonald Cornford, *The Unwritten Philosophy and Other Essays* (Cambridge: Cambridge University Press, 1950), 83–88.

3. See Alfred North Whitehead, *Science and the Modern World: Lowell Lectures, 1925* (New York: Macmillan, 1925).

4. Friedrich Nietzsche, *Twilight of the Idols, The Anti-Christ*, trans. R. J. Hollingdale (New York: Penguin, 1968), 33.

5. Karl Popper locates the origin of the Marxist party in the state that was under the sovereignty of the Platonic philosopher/king and the origin of the state in the theocracy of Egypt. See Popper's *The Open Society and Its Enemies* (London: Routledge, 1945).

6. Sigmund Freud, *Moses and Monotheism*, trans. Katherine Jones (New York: Vintage, 1939).

7. Friedrich Nietzsche, *Philosophy in the Tragic Age of the Greeks*, trans. Marianne Cowan (Chicago: Regnery, Gateway ed., 1962).

8. Friedrich Nietzsche, "On Truth and Lying," *Friedrich Nietzsche on Rhetoric and Language*, ed. and trans. Sander L. Gilman, Carole Blair, and David J. Parent (New York: Oxford University Press, 1989), 250–251.

Two **The Status of Form**

1. Jacques Derrida, *Edmund Husserl's "Origin of Geometry": An Introduction*, trans. John P. Leavey, Jr. (incl. Husserl's "Origin of Geometry," trans. David Carr) (Lincoln: University of Nebraska Press, 1962).

2. Edmund Husserl, *The Crisis of European Sciences and Transcendental Phenomenology*, trans. David Carr (Evanston: Northwestern University Press, 1970), 48–49.

3. Edmund Husserl, *Logical Investigations*, vol. 1, trans. J. N. Findlay (London: Routledge & Kegan Paul, 1982), 244.

4. Husserl, *Logical Investigations*, vol. 1, 244.

5. Ibid., 353.

6. Ibid., 350.

7. Ibid., 350.

8. Martin Heidegger, "The End of Philosophy and the Task of Thinking," *Basic Writings*, ed. David F. Krell (New York: Harper & Row, 1977), 374.

9. Ibid., 376.

10. Ibid., 378.

11. Translator's note: Although *ab-gründig* also means abyssal, and *Ab-gründlichkeit* "abyssalness," I chose to use "ungrounded-ness" in order to conserve the nuance carried in the Japanese translation of the word, which the author stresses. Please refer to Martin Heidegger, *Nietzsche*, vol. 4: *Nihilism*, trans. Frank A. Capuzzi (San Francisco: Harper & Row, 1982), 193.

Three Architecture and Poetry

1. Paul Valéry, *Eupalinos, or the Architect*, trans. William M. Stewart (London: Oxford University Press, 1932).

2. Paul Valéry, "Man and Sea Shell," in *The Collected Works of Paul Valéry*, vol. 1, selected with an introduction by James R. Lawler (Princeton: Princeton University Press, 1956), 117.

3. Ibid., 119.

4. Paul Valéry, "Reflections on Art," in *Collected Works of Paul Valéry*, vol. 13, trans. Ralph Manheim (New York: Pantheon, 1964), 145–146.

Four The Natural City

1. Christopher Alexander, "A City Is Not a Tree," *Architectural Forum*, 122, no. 1 (April 1965), 58.

2. Ibid., 58–59, emphasis added.

3. Ibid., 59.

4. Ibid., 59.

5. Christopher Alexander, "A City Is Not a Tree, Part 2," *Architectural Forum*, 122, no. 2 (May 1965), 61.

Five **Structure and Zero**

1. Ferdinand de Saussure, *Course in General Linguistics*, trans. Wade Baskin (New York: McGraw–Hill, 1959), 120.

2. Roman Jakobson, *Six Lectures on Sound and Meaning*, trans. John Mepham (Cambridge, Mass.: MIT Press, 1978), 81.

3. Claude Lévi-Strauss, *Structural Anthropology*, trans. Claire Jacobson and Brooke Schoepf (New York: Basic, 1963), 33.

4. Jakobson, *Six Lectures on Sound and Meaning*, 74.

5. R. Jakobson and J. Lotz, "Notes on the French Phonemic Pattern," *Roman Jakobson, Selected Writings*, vol. 1, *Phonological Studies*, 2d ed. (Paris: Mouton, 1971), 431.

6. Stéphane Mallarmé, "Sur Poe" in "Proses diverses, réponses à des enquêtes," *Oeuvres complètes*, ed. Henri Mondor and G. Jean-Aubry (Paris: Gallimard, 1951), 872.

7. Lao-Tzu, *Te-Tao Ching*, trans. Robert G. Hendricks (New York: Ballantine, 1989), 63.

8. Gilles Deleuze, "A quoi reconnaît-on le structuralisme?," *La Philosophie au XXe Siècle*, vol. 4, sous la direction de François Châtelet (Paris: Librairie Hachette, 1973), 300.

9. Claude Lévi-Strauss, *Introduction to the Work of Marcel Mauss*, trans. Felicity Baker (London: Routledge & Kegan Paul, 1987), 55.

10. Shinran, *Tan ni sho: A Shin Buddhist Classic*, trans. Taitetsu Unno (Honolulu: Buddhist Study Center Press, 1984). Shinran (1173–1262) released Japanese Buddhism from all the magico-religious factors and founded Jodo Shin Shu, to which the majority of Japanese Buddhists belong.

11. Roland Barthes, *The Empire of Signs*, trans. Richard Howard (New York: Hill, 1982).

Six **Natural Numbers**
1. Paul de Man, "The Epistemology of Metaphor," *On Metaphor*, ed. Sheldon Sacks (Chicago: University of Chicago Press, 1978), 14.

2. Paul de Man, *Allegories of Reading: Figural Language in Rousseau, Nietzsche, Rilke, and Proust* (New Haven: Yale University Press, 1979), 4.

3. Morris Kline, *Mathematics: The Loss of Certainty* (New York: Oxford University Press, 1980).

Seven **Natural Language**
1. De Man, *Allegories of Reading*, 17.

Eight **Money**
1. Karl Marx, *Capital*, vol. 1, trans. Ben Fowkes (New York: Vintage, 1976), 125. Emphasis added.

2. Ibid., 140.

3. Ibid., 156.

4. Marx writes: "Es ist als ob neben und ausser Löwen, Tigern, Hasen und allen andern wirklichen Thieren, die gruppirt die verschiednen Geschlechter, Arten, Unterarten, Familien u.s.w. des Thierreichs bilden, auch noch das Thier existirte, die individuelle Incarnation des ganzen Thierreichs." See Karl Marx, *Das Kapital: Kritik der politischen Oekonomie*, vol. 1 (Hamburg: O. Meissner; New York: L. W. Schmidt, 1867–1894), 27.

Nine **Natural Intelligence**
1. De Man, *Allegories of Reading*, 9–10.

2. Gregory Bateson, *Steps to an Ecology of Mind* (New York: Ballantine, 1972), 202–203.

3. Ibid., 209.

4. See chapter 1 in Gilles Deleuze and Félix Guattari, *Anti-Oedipus: Capitalism and Schizophrenia* (Minneapolis: University of Minnesota Press, 1983).

Ten **Schismogenesis**

1. Jane Jacobs, *The Economy of Cities* (New York: Vintage, 1970), 3.

2. Ibid., 66.

3. Ibid., 58, diagram indicating four additions to *D*.

4. Ibid., 59.

5. Ibid., 5.

6. Frederick Engels, "Socialism: Utopian and Scientific," *Karl Marx and Frederick Engels: Selected Works* (Moscow: Progress Publishers, 1968), 413.

7. Vladimir I. Lenin, *One Step Forward, Two Steps Back: The Crisis in Our Party* (Moscow: Progress Publishers, 1947).

8. Marx and Engels, *The German Ideology, Part One*, 89.

9. Ibid., 54.

10. Ibid., 51–52.

11. Jacobs, *The Economy of Cities*, 62.

Eleven **Being**

1. Friedrich Nietzsche, *The Will to Power*, trans. Walter Kaufmann and R. J. Hollingdale (New York: Vintage, 1967), 270.

2. Claude Lévi-Strauss, *The Elementary Structures of Kinship*, trans. James Harle Bell and John Richard Von Sturmer, ed. Rodney Needham (Boston: Beacon Press, 1969), 24–25.

3. Ibid., 25.

4. Nietzsche writes: "The strange family resemblance of all Indian, Greek, and German philosophizing is explained easily

enough. Where there is affinity of languages, it cannot fail, owing to the common philosophy of grammar—I mean, owing to the unconscious domination and guidance by similar grammatical functions—that everything is prepared at the outset for a similar development and sequence of philosophical systems; just as the way seems barred against certain other possibilities of world-interpretation. It is highly probable that philosophers within the domain of the Ural-Altaic languages (where the concept of the subject is least developed) look otherwise "into the world," and will be found on paths of thought different from those of the Indo-Germanic peoples and the Muslims: the spell of certain grammatical functions is ultimately also the spell of *physiological* valuations and racial conditions." From *Nietzsche's Beyond Good and Evil: Prelude to a Philosophy of the Future*, trans. Walter Kaufmann (New York: Vintage, 1966), 27–28.

5. Martin Heidegger, *Nietzsche*, vol. 4: *Nihilism*, trans. Frank A. Capuzzi (San Francisco: Harper & Row, 1982), 194–195.

6. Ibid., 193.

Twelve **The Formalization of Philosophy**

1. Chaim Perelman, *The Realm of Rhetoric*, trans. William Kluback (Notre Dame: University of Notre Dame Press, 1982), 127–128.

2. Ibid., 130.

3. Jacques Derrida, "The Supplement of Copula: Philosophy before Linguistics," *Margins of Philosophy*, trans. Alan Bass (Chicago: University of Chicago Press, 1982), 177.

4. Louis Althusser, "Lenin and Philosophy," *Philosophy and the Spontaneous Philosophy of the Scientists*, ed. Gregory Elliot (London: Verso, 1989), 192.

5. Ibid., 194.

Thirteen **Solipsism**

1. Wittgenstein, *Remarks on the Foundations of Mathematics*, 383.

2. Ibid., 388.

3. Plato, "Meno," *The Collected Dialogues of Plato, Including the Letters*, Bollingen Series LXXI, ed. Edith Hamilton and Huntington Cairns (Princeton: Princeton University Press, 1961), 366.

4. Nicholas Rescher, *Dialectics: A Controversy-Oriented Approach to the Theory of Knowledge* (Albany: State University of New York Press, 1977).

5. Plato, "Meno," *The Collected Dialogues of Plato*, 368.

Fourteen **The Standpoint of Teaching**

1. Wittgenstein, *Philosophical Investigations*, 9e.

2. Marx, *Capital*, vol. 1, 200–201.

3. Wittgenstein, *Philosophical Investigations*, 81e.

4. Saul A. Kripke, "The Wittgensteinian Paradox," *Wittgenstein on Rules and Private Language: An Elementary Exposition* (Cambridge, Mass.: Harvard University Press, 1982), 21.

5. Ludwig F. Wittgenstein, *Tractatus Logico-Philosophicus*, trans. C. K. Ogden (London: Routledge & Kegan Paul, 1992), 189.

6. Allan Janik and Stephen Toulmin, *Wittgenstein's Vienna* (New York: Simon & Schuster, 1973), 169.

7. Saul A. Kripke, "The Solution and the 'Private Language' Argument," *Wittgenstein on Rules and Private Language*, 55.

8. Marx, *Capital*, vol. 1, 163.

Fifteen **Architecture as Metaphor**

1. Wittgenstein, *Philosophical Investigations*, 39e.

2. Wittgenstein, *Remarks on the Foundations of Mathematics*, part 3, #46, 176–177.

3. Ibid., part 3, #1, 143.

4. Ibid., part 3, #2, 143.

5. Ibid., part 3, #42, 173.

6. Ibid., part 3, #46, 176.

7. Ibid., part 1, #166, 99.

8. Ibid., part 2, #2, 111.

9. Ibid., part 3, #46, 176.

10. Wittgenstein, *Philosophical Investigations*, 32e.

11. Ibid., 31e.

Sixteen **On Rules**

1. Wittgenstein, *Philosophical Investigations*, 85e.

2. Plato, "Meno," *The Collected Dialogues of Plato*, 364.

3. Wittgenstein, *Philosophical Investigations*, 12e.

4. Wittgenstein, *Remarks on the Foundations of Mathematics*, 209.

5. Wittgenstein, *Philosophical Investigations*, 81e.

6. Jacques Derrida, *Speech and Phenomena and Other Essays on Husserl's Theory of Signs*, trans. David B. Allison (Evanston: Northwestern University Press, 1973), 79–80.

7. Ibid., 67.

8. F. A. Hayek, *Law, Legislation, and Liberty*, vol. 1: *Rules and Order* (Chicago: University of Chicago Press, 1973), 46–47.

Seventeen **Society and Community**

1. Marx, *Capital*, vol. 1, 182.

2. Ibid., 471–472.

3. Ibid., 164–165.

4. Ibid., 166–167.

Eighteen **The Linguistic Turn and *Cogito***

1. Saul A. Kripke, *Naming and Necessity* (Cambridge, Mass.: Harvard University Press, 1972).

2. This kind of critique would not understand the later Wittgenstein as an exponent of this language-centered approach; it should be remembered that in this period Wittgenstein attempted to criticize formalism in the broadest sense. For him, a "linguistic turn" no longer made sense; the *Tractatus*, which came from his early period, had already attempted such a turn. It was his self-determined task in the later period to criticize it.

3. Rescher, *Dialectics*, 58, 94–95.

4. Ibid., 60.

Nineteen **Selling**

1. Sigmund Freud, *The Complete Introductory Lectures on Psychoanalysis*, trans. James Strachey (New York: W. W. Norton, 1966), 447.

2. Marx, *Capital*, vol. 1, 166–167.

3. Ibid., 151. Marx quotes from Aristotle, *Nicomachean Ethics* (London: Loeb, 1926), bk. 5, ch. 5, 287–289.

4. Marx, *Capital*, vol. 1, 151.

5. Ibid., 147.

6. Ibid., 139–140.

7. Ibid., 140.

8. Ibid., 149–150.

9. Ibid., 187.

10. It is important to note that Marx's theory of the fetishism of commodity is qualitatively different from the idea of "reification" developed by Georg Lukács, which continues to be important for many contemporary thinkers. Unlike reification, which derived from Marx's concept of commodity—that it "reflects the social relation of the producers . . . as a social relation between objects"—*Capital* scrutinizes how such a "relation" works. There is no rational basis for exchange, and thus the selling position constantly requires a "fatal leap." For this

reason, the theory of "reification" as such cannot access the totality of *Capital*, in particular the dynamic movement of capital that is instigated by crises.

Twenty **Merchant Capital**

1. Marx, *Capital*, vol. 1, 176.

2. Max Weber emphasized the difference between merchant and industrial capital, stressing that the "rationality" of industrial capital had once been motivated by an irrational "asceticism" (Protestantism).

3. Marx, *Capital*, vol. 1, 211–212.

4. Kojin Karatani, *Marx: The Center of His Possibilities* (Tokyo: Kodansha, 1978).

5. Marx, *Capital*, vol. 1, 254–255.

Twenty-one **Credit**

1. Marx, *Capital*, vol. 1, 236–237.

2. Søren Kierkegaard, *Practice in Christianity*, ed. and trans. Howard V. Hong and Edna H. Hong (Princeton: Princeton University Press, 1991), 36.

3. Marx and Engels, *The German Ideology, Part One*, 56–57. In the English translation, "abolishes" was used for the term *aufhebt*. Although it represents one aspect of the term, it excludes others, such as "to pick up something from the ground, to stop or undo something, and to synthesize." In English it is most often translated as "sublates."

Afterword

1. Karl Marx, "A Contribution to the Critique of Hegel's Philosophy of Right," *Early Writings*, trans. Rodney Livingstone and Gregor Benton (New York: Vintage, 1975), 257. Here the same term as above, *Aufhebung*, is translated "transcendence."

2. Ibid., 244.

3. Ibid., 243.

Illustration Credits

Page 30: Redrawn from Christopher Alexander, "A City Is Not a Tree, Part 2," *Architectural Forum*, 122, no. 2 (May 1965), 60.

Pages 32, 33, and 35: Redrawn from Christopher Alexander, "A City Is Not a Tree," *Architectural Forum*, 122, no. 1 (April 1965), 59, 62.

Page 62: Redrawn from Kojin Karatani, *Introspection and Retrospection* (Tokyo: Kodansha, 1988), 135.

Page 82: Redrawn from Jane Jacobs, *The Economy of Cities* (New York: Vintage, 1970), 58.